The Entertainer

A Play

John Osborne

Music by
John Addison

Samuel French – London
New York – Sydney – Toronto – Hollywood

The Entertainer

A Play

John Osborne

Music by
John Addison

Samuel French – London
New York – Sydney – Toronto – Hollywood

The Entertainer

This play was first presented by The English Stage Company at The Royal Court Theatre, London, on 10th April 1957, with the following cast:—

BILLIE RICE	George Relph
JEAN RICE	Dorothy Tutin
PHOEBE RICE	Brenda de Banzie
ARCHIE RICE	Laurence Olivier
FRANK RICE	Richard Pasco
GORGEOUS GLADYS	Vivienne Drummond
WILLIAM (BROTHER BILL) RICE	Aubrey Dexter
GRAHAM	Stanley Meadows

and subsequently by The English Stage Company, in association with Laurence Olivier Productions, at The Palace Theatre, London, on 10th September 1957, with the following cast:—

BILLIE RICE	George Relph
JEAN RICE	Joan Plowright
PHOEBE RICE	Brenda de Banzie
ARCHIE RICE	Laurence Olivier
FRANK RICE	Richard Pascoe
BRITANNIA	Jennifer Wallace
WILLIAM (BROTHER BILL) RICE	Albert Chevalier
GRAHAM	Robert Stephens

Settings by ALAN TAGG *with costumes by* CLARE JEFFREY

Music by JOHN ADDISON

Directed by TONY RICHARDSON

No character, in this play, is intended to portray any specific person, alive or dead. Running time of this play, excluding intervals, is approximately two hours.

The Entertainer

THIS play was first presented by The English Stage Company at The Royal Court Theatre, London, on 10th April 1957, with the following cast:—

BILLIE RICE	George Relph
JEAN RICE	Dorothy Tutin
PHOEBE RICE	Brenda de Banzie
ARCHIE RICE	Laurence Olivier
FRANK RICE	Richard Pasco
GORGEOUS GLADYS	Vivienne Drummond
WILLIAM (BROTHER BILL) RICE	Aubrey Dexter
GRAHAM	Stanley Meadows

and subsequently by The English Stage Company, in association with Laurence Olivier Productions, at The Palace Theatre, London, on 10th September 1957, with the following cast:—

BILLIE RICE	George Relph
JEAN RICE	Joan Plowright
PHOEBE RICE	Brenda de Banzie
ARCHIE RICE	Laurence Olivier
FRANK RICE	Richard Pascoe
BRITANNIA	Jennifer Wallace
WILLIAM (BROTHER BILL) RICE	Albert Chevalier
GRAHAM	Robert Stephens

Settings by ALAN TAGG with costumes by CLARE JEFFREY

Music by JOHN ADDISON

Directed by TONY RICHARDSON

No character, in this play, is intended to portray any specific person, alive or dead. Running time of this play, excluding intervals, is approximately two hours.

PRODUCTION NOTE

Here is a view of England seen through the eyes of a music-hall comedian and his family, and constructed with the disciplined freedom of the twice nightly variety programme.

As the challenge to the director and cast is considerable, it is assumed you will not be attempting this play unless you have responded to and been stimulated by it. Therefore these few production notes are intended to guide the group over the pitfalls and not to explain or justify the play's philosophy; as such they will be as severely practical as possible.

John Osborne has said that he wants to make people *feel* in the theatre, and let them think afterwards. His method is to throw before the audience statements, ideas and situations, and then let them respond at their will. During performances at the Royal Court Theatre the casts of *Look Back in Anger* and *The Entertainer* used to play a game of guessing where some members of the audience would walk out. Indeed, Mr. Osborne, in his Foreword to the Acting Edition of *Look Back in Anger* (q.v.), postulates that for members of an audience to leave the theatre is a response: better they should leave noisily, because they have been offended, than sit snug and unhearing.

Like all plays written by actors, from Shakespeare onwards, *The Entertainer* has dialogue which only works to its greatest effect when spoken to a listening audience. The construction and punctuation of the dialogue is dramatic and not literary. Observe, for instance, the difference in rhythm between Billy's opening speech in Number Five and Archie's closing lines: the one broad and flowing; the other nervous and jerky. You may examine the whole play in this way.

Staging

The place is England—the time is 1956.

Alan Tagg's original settings for the Royal Court Theatre had a two-fold intention: (1) that the settings could be changed without any pause in the presentation (of course, John Osborne's construction of the play enormously helps this) and (2) that the whole play should have the atmosphere of the music-hall. Accordingly, false stage boxes were designed for the Royal Court Theatre with heavily decorated bow fronts topped with red plush, the usual theatre front curtain was replaced by an example of a typical music-hall advertisement cloth, and electrically operated numerical indicators were installed which lit up and showed the number of each "turn" as it was being played.

Directly behind the advertisement cloth was the music-hall area: tormentors either side, through which Archie Rice entered or left, and a gaudily painted gauze backdrop. This gauze was backed with black "tabs" so that scenery and property changes could be carried out behind the gauze backdrop while a music-hall number was being played in front. A rising microphone was installed to come up at the footlights for the music-hall scenes.

When the gauze and its attendant black tabs were flown out, the Rices' living-room was revealed. Even here the music-hall atmosphere was retained. No naturalistic room with the fourth wall removed, but gauze wings, gauze back-drop (the top of which could be seen by the audience) and heavily swagged borders. In this backdrop was set the living room door, which opened onstage showing the passage beyond, and which was reached by stairs coming up through the stage. There was no backing to the stairs or passage except the back wall of the theatre. (See frontispiece, also ground plan facing p. 16.)

Because the gauze wings could not act as masking in themselves, plum-coloured velvet legs were also hung at the necessary intervals up each side.

The use of gauze, which is difficult material to paint, hang and light, is *not* essential to the play. Because Alan Tagg used it, it meant that at the Royal Court Theatre it was possible, with appropriate lighting, to see the back wall, although the music-hall backdrop and the living-room backdrop were both "in"; as far as the living-room backdrop was concerned it meant that artists could be seen coming up the stairs and walking along the passage to the living-room door: and for the music-hall backdrop it meant that the nude posing as Britannia in Number Nine could be set behind the backdrop (and its black tabs) during the music-hall scene and to reveal the nude only necessitated the black tabs being drawn aside and the lighting being changed. The back wall of the theatre was used twice, once at the beginning of the play when it was hung with neon and bright electric signs to represent a street, and once at the very end of the play when the entire stage was cleared completely and it represented itself—the backwall of a theatre.

This description has been dealt with at some length in the hope that it might help by knowing how the original production was planned scenically. It can, of course, be simplified. There are three areas necessary: the orchestra pit, the music-hall, and the sitting-room. The music-hall needs three to four feet in depth, after which the remainder of the stage area (not forgetting to allow for the music-hall backdrop) can be given to the living-room. There is *no need* to see beyond the living room backdrop, and the door can lead off right or left to save having to allow for the depth of a passage outside the door. The stage left tormentor opening was used at the Royal Court as the entrance to Phoebe's kitchen, so it is conceivable that the stage right tormentor opening could be the door to the living-room. An entrance far down stage is not easy to use from the producer's point of view, but this alternative might be considered a better entrance for the artists than entering through the wings, if this form of staging is used.

It must be remembered that the Rice family can play over the music-hall area, so that the living-room scenes can be opened out, but of course the

artists must be moved upstage of the music-hall backdrop before the end of the scene. This linking of the two areas is particularly useful between Numbers eight to nine and nine to ten, when Archie Rice goes directly from the room into his music-hall turn, and at the end of the turn is immediately part of the living-room scene once more.

Some short notes on the characters

Very few words are needed on the characters. John Osborne has written his own notes about them and, with those in mind while a careful study is made of the text, each character is found to have a past as well as a present. Even Brother Bill and Graham, although their *rôles* are very small—and although their scenes are concurrent, switching from one side of the stage where Jean and Graham play their scene on the same settee that has been used all through the play, to the other side where a desk and two chairs have replaced Billie's armchair—they are both characters who have been mentioned many times during the course of the play. Not only do their scenes add greatly to our knowledge of the destinies of Archie and Jean, but they also complement all that has been said about themselves.

In thinking of Billie Rice, one can but quote John Osborne writing in the programme for the Boston U.S.A. opening: "The only way he could deal with life was continually to draw on the strength of his remembered past".

Between Jean and Frank—a half brother and sister—there is a deep affection, understanding and tolerance. It is this same tolerance, as well as her intelligence, that allows Jean to accept Phoebe's attitude in Number Eight and it is to Phoebe that she gives unspoken comfort in Number Ten. Frank plays at being Archie's "feed", until the news of Mick's death strikes right through the gay *façade* we have seen up till then.

Finally, Phoebe and Archie Rice: both wonderful acting parts with tremendous scope and variety; each knowingly acting a part, but each being caught off guard, for example, with Phoebe in Number Seven and with Archie in Number Ten.

Music

Music for *The Entertainer* has been specially composed by John Addison and is available on hire direct *from the Publishers only*. They will be glad to furnish particulars on request.

The work is scored for viola, B♭ trumpet, trombone, percussion and piano. When all these instruments are not available it is desirable that at least a percussion player be used with a piano.

NOTE

The music hall is dying, and, with it, a significant part of England. Some of the heart of England has gone; something that once belonged to everyone, for this was truly a folk art. In writing this play, I have not used some of the techniques of the music hall in order to exploit an effective trick, but because I believe that these can solve some of the eternal problems of time and space that face the dramatist and, also, it has been relevant to the story and setting. Not only has this technique its own traditions, its own convention and symbol, its own mystique, it cuts right across the restrictions of the so-called naturalistic stage. Its contact is immediate, vital and direct.

CAST

BILLY RICE

JEAN RICE

PHOEBE RICE

ARCHIE RICE

FRANK RICE

WILLIAM (BROTHER BILL) RICE

GRAHAM DODD

and

BRITANNIA

OVERTURE

1. Billy and Jean.
2. Archie Rice—"Don't take him seriously!"
3. Billy, Jean and Phoebe.
4. Archie Rice—"In Trouble Again".
5. Billy, Jean, Phoebe and Archie.

INTERMISSION

6. Billy, Phoebe, Jean, Archie and Frank.
7. Archie Rice—"Interrupts the Programme".
8. Billy, Phoebe, Jean, Archie and Frank.

INTERMISSION

9. Frank Rice—"Singing for You".
10. Billy, Phoebe, Jean, Archie and Frank.
11. The Good Old Days Again.
12. Jean and Graham—Archie and Brother Bill.
13. Archie Rice—"The One and Only".

Woolworth's now, did I tell you? I'm on the electrical counter. It's not bad. Girls are a bit common, that's all. Oh, it is nice to see you. Archie will be so pleased. She looks a bit peeky. Round the face, don't you think? Don't you think she looks a bit peeky?

BILLY. She looks all right.

PHOEBE. I don't suppose she's eating properly. You know what these young girls are. They worry about their figures. So, you didn't go away for the weekend after all?

JEAN. No.

PHOEBE. Graham's all right, is he?

JEAN. Yes, he's all right.

PHOEBE. There's nothing wrong there, is there?

BILLY. Why don't you mind your bloody business? She'll tell you if she wants to.

PHOEBE. All right, I know. She doesn't mind telling me if there's anything, do you?

JEAN. We had a slight disagreement. Nothing more, that's all.

PHOEBE. After all, she may not be my own, but I did help to bring her up a little, didn't I? After all, she's Archie's daughter. Be a bit strange if I wasn't interested whether she was happy or not. Oh, well, dear, don't take any notice. You'll soon make it up. Men are funny. You don't want to take any notice of them.

JEAN (smiling). Wish I didn't.

PHOEBE. That's right. Have another drink. You'll soon feel better. What did you have a row about? Something silly, I bet. You haven't broken off your engagement?

JEAN. I don't know. Probably.

PHOEBE. Oh dear, I'm sorry.

JEAN. I went to the Rally in Trafalgar Square last Sunday.

BILLY. What for, for God's sake?

JEAN. Because, Grandad, somehow—with a whole lot of other people, strange as it may seem—I managed to get myself steamed up about the way things were going.

BILLY. And you went to Trafalgar Square?

PHOEBE. Well, she said so, didn't she?

BILLY. Well, I should think you want your bloody head read!

JEAN. That was more or less Graham's feelings about it. Only he happens to be about fifty years younger than you, and he put it a bit differently. It all really started over something I wanted to do, and then it all came out, lots of things. All kinds of bitterness—things I didn't even know existed.

BILLY. I didn't know you were interested in politics.

JEAN. Neither did I. I've always found the whole thing rather boring.

BILLY. Good God! I've heard some things in my time: This is what comes of giving them the bloody vote. They start breaking off their engagements, just because they believe every shiftless lay-about writing for the papers.

PHOEBE. Oh, shut up, just for a minute, Dad. You had a row because of something you wanted to do?

JEAN. Well, it's—oh, it's a complicated story. I think I wrote and told you I was teaching art to a bunch of youth club kids?

PHOEBE. Oh, yes. That was ages ago.

JEAN. Nearly a year. I knew someone who had been doing it—a young man Graham knew. He said it was too much for him, and he couldn't stick it any longer. "They're little bastards, the lot of them," he said. "If anyone believes you can teach those monsters to create anything, they're crazy. They're not even barbarians—they haven't got the charm for that. They're just plain, dim, nasty savages. They'll kill us all if they can." That's what he said. But—something, something, made me want to have a go at it. There wasn't any money in it. Just a few shillings for a few nights a week. But it was something I knew a little about—or thought I knew about. I'd never been good enough to do anything myself, but I thought this was something I wanted to do. Even if it was just battling a gang of moronic teenagers. The club leader thought I was mad, and so did Graham.

PHOEBE. I can't say I blame him really. It doesn't sound a very nice job at all. Not for a young girl like you, Jean. They sound like a real tough crowd to me.

JEAN. They were. Too tough for either of the young men who had taken them on before.

PHOEBE. Well, if they don't want to learn, why do they go, for heaven's sake?

JEAN. It was an obligatory class, if they attended one of my classes a week, they could take part in the club's other activities, the dances and so on. I fought those kids back, and some of them were eight feet tall. Most of the time I've loathed it, and I loathed them. I pretended to myself that I didn't, but I did. I hated them, and I

think I was getting somewhere. And now Graham wants me to marry him. Now, before he's qualified. But I wouldn't. He doesn't want me to try something for myself. He doesn't want me to threaten him or his world, he doesn't want me to succeed. I refused him. Then it all came out—Trafalgar Square and everything. You know, I hadn't realized: it just hadn't occurred to me that you could love somebody, that you could want them, and want them twenty-four hours of the day and then suddenly find that you're neither of you even living in the same world. I don't understand that. I just don't understand it. I wish I could understand it. It's frightening. Sorry, Phoebe, I shouldn't be drinking your gin. I bought this for you.

BILLY. Well, we only need a few pigeons for it to be like Trafalgar Square in here. I've never known such a draughty bloody place. Everybody leaves the windows and doors open. I don't believe that's healthy. I tell you, you come in one door and you get blown out the other.

JEAN. How's young Mick? Have you heard from him?

PHOEBE. Oh, yes. Of course. He's out there—you knew that, didn't you?

JEAN. Yes. I knew.

PHOEBE. Archie worries about him. He doesn't say so, but I know he does. It's funny really because they never seemed to hit it off so well, in lots of ways. Not like you and him, or Frank. He's a very sensible boy, young Mick. He's very straight. I've lost some sleep this week, I can tell you.

BILLY. He's a fine boy. When they called him, he went. No arguments, nothing. He just went.

JEAN (suddenly). And when they called Frank he refused, and he went to jail for it—for six months. Young Frank full of doubts about himself, and everybody, with a cold in his head half the year, and a weak chest. Lucky to pass C3. Poor Frank. (To PHOEBE.) He's not very strong, you always said. You went without to buy him little luxuries to eat; why, you wouldn't let him even clean his own shoes. No, you'd do it for him. But he went and said no, and, what's more, he went to jail for it. Oh, he gave in eventually, but he said no for six months of his poor protected life—he said no! I think that's something. You don't have to measure up young Mick against Frank, Grandad. Now, don't look hurt. I'm not getting at you. I love you very much, both of you, but I probably shouldn't have started drinking gin on the train.

(*Pause.*)

PHOEBE. Well, we'll shut up about it now.

BILLY. I just said that Mick was a good boy.

JEAN. He is. He's a very good boy. He's a gallant young nineteen year old who's fighting for us all, who never somehow learnt to say no, who never wanted to, and I hope to God he comes back safely.

PHOEBE. Oh, dear, Jean, you think he'll be all right, don't you? I don't know why they send these boys out to do the fighting. They're just kids, that's all. That's all he is, a kid.

BILLY. You can't turn against your own people, Jean. You can't do it.

JEAN. Where is Frank? My own people—who are my people?

PHOEBE. He plays the piano in one of these late-night drinking places. It's not bad. I went along there one night. Just a lot of people standing around drinking. I've never been one for going out to drink. I'd rather have it at home. It's something for him to do. He doesn't seem to know what to do with himself. Since he came out of that place. That damned prison. I'll never forget it. Making him go to prison. I'll never forget it. I can't get over it—ever.

JEAN. Well, it's all over now. Have some more of that gin. I bought it for you.

PHOEBE. I won't. And making him do that job. A boy like him shouldn't be doing it. Hospital porter. D'you know they make him stoke the boilers?

JEAN. Yes. He'd have been better off in the Army—sticking a bayonet into some wog.

PHOEBE. He doesn't say a word to me about it. I wish he hadn't done it, all the same. I wonder whether Mick isn't better off after all. I mean, they do look after them, don't they?

JEAN. Oh, yes, they look after them all right.

BILLY. Look after them better now than they did, when I was in it. I haven't read the evening paper yet. The Dardanelles—I went through that without a scratch. Not a scratch on me.

JEAN. They're all looking after us. We're all right, all of us. Nothing to worry about. *We're* all right. God save the Queen!

(*Blackout. Draw tabs.*)

NUMBER FOUR

Spotlight on ARCHIE *at microphone.*

ARCHIE. I've played in front of them all! "The Queen", "The Duke of Edinburgh", "The Prince of Wales", and the—what's the name of that other pub? Blimey, that went better first house. (*Pause.*) I've taken my glasses off. I don't want to see you suffering. What about these crooners, eh? What about these crooners? I don't know what we're coming to. I don't, honest. Look at the stuff they sing. Look at the songs they sing! "The Dark Town Strutters' Ball", "The Woodchoppers' Ball", "The Basin Street Ball"—it's a lot of rubbish, isn't it? I'll bet you thought I was a rotten act before I came on, didn't you? What about these girls? (*Indicates* U.S.) What about them? Smashin'! I bet you think I have a marvellous time up here with all these posing girls, don't you? You think I have a smashin' time, don't you? (*Pause.*) You're dead right! You wouldn't think I was sexy to look at me, would you! No, lady, I mean it. To look at me you wouldn't think I was sexy, would you! (*Pause.*) You ask him! (*Points to conductor's stand.*) Ask him! (*Staring out at audience.*) You think I'm like that, don't you? You think I am! Well, I'm not. But *he* is! (*Points to conductor's stand again.*) I'd rather have a glass of beer any day! And now I'm going to sing you a little song, a little song, a little song written by the wife's sister, a little song entitled "The Old Church bell won't ring to-night, as the Vicar's dropped a Clanger". Thank you, Charlie.

We're all out for good old number one,
Number one's the only one for me!
Good old England, you're my cup of tea,
But I don't want no drab equality.
Don't let your feelings roam,
But remember that charity begins at home.
For Britons shall be free! For Britons shall be free!
The National Health won't bring you wealth
Those wigs and blooming spectacles are bought by you and me.
The Army, and the Navy and the Air Force,
Are all we need to make the blighters see
It still belongs to you, the old red, white and blue.
(*Drop Union Flag.*)

Those bits of red still on the map
We won't give up without a scrap.
What we've got left back
We'll keep—and blow you, Jack!
Oh, number one's the only one for me!
We're all out for good old number one;
Yes, number one's the only one for me—
God bless you!
Number one's the only one for me! *(Ad lib—see score.)*
              (Exit.)

NUMBER FIVE

BILLY, JEAN, PHOEBE AND ARCHIE

BILLY. They were graceful, they had mystery and dignity. Why,
when a woman got out of a cab, she descended. Descended. And
you put your hand out to her smartly to help her down. Look at
them today. Have you ever seen a woman get out of a car? Well,
have you? I have, and I don't want to see it again, thank you very
much. Why I never saw a woman's legs until I was nineteen. Didn't
know what they looked like. Nineteen. I was married when I was
nineteen, you know. I was only twenty when Archie's brother
was born. Old Bill. He's got on, anyway. I remember the first
time I set eyes on your grandmother. She was just eighteen. She
had a velvet coat on, black it was, black with fur round the edge.
They were all the fashion just about then. It was so tight round her
figure. And with her little fur cap on and muff, she looked a picture.
      *(ARCHIE rushes in, his arms full with a carrier bag and bottles,
briskly distracted. ARCHIE RICE is about fifty. His hair is brushed flat,
almost grey. He wears glasses and has a slight stoop, from a kind of
inverted pedantry which he originally assumed thirty years ago when he
left one of those minor public day schools in London, which have usually
managed to produce some raffish middle class adventurers as well as
bank managers and poets. Landladies adore and cosset him because he
is so friendly, and obviously such a gentleman. Some of his fellow
artists even call him "Professor" occasionally, as they might call a
retired army captain "Colonel". He smiles kindly at this simplicity,
knowing himself to belong to no class and plays the part as well as he*

knows how. He lightly patronizes his father, whom he admires deeply. He patronizes his wife, PHOEBE, whom he pities wholeheartedly. It is this which has prevented him from leaving her twenty years ago. Or, is it simply because, as many people would suggest, he lacks the courage? Anyway, he makes no secret of his perennial affairs with other women— real and fictitious. It is part of his pity, part of his patronage, part of his personal myth. He patronizes his elder son, Frank, who lacks his own brand of indulgence, stoicism and bravura, and for whom he has an almost unreal, pantomime affection. In contrast, his patronage of his daughter, Jean, is more wary, sly, unsure. He suspects her intelligence, aware that she may be stronger than the rest of them. Whatever he says to anyone is almost always very carefully "thrown away". Apparently absent minded, it is a comedian's technique, it absolves him from seeming committed to anyone or anything.)

ARCHIE. Hello, women's legs again! (*To the others.*) That's what Sterne calls riding your tit with sobriety. I think it was Sterne anyway. Or was it George Robey? Um? Hello, dear, this is nice. (*He kisses* JEAN.) I haven't got my glasses on. I thought you were the income tax man sitting there. I thought we had shaken him off. All right, are you?

JEAN. Thank you. I have had too much gin waiting for you.

ARCHIE. Never mind, you can have some more in a minute. You haven't fixed an hotel or anything respectable, have you?

JEAN. No, but—

ARCHIE. Jolly good. I'm sleeping alone tonight. The back of my legs ache as it is. You and Phoebe can sleep up in my room, and I'll kip on the sofa. I've just been talking to our coloured friend on the stairs.

PHOEBE. He's a student.

ARCHIE. No, he's not. He's a ballet dancer.

PHOEBE (*astonished*). Is he! (*To* JEAN.) He's a big fellow.

ARCHIE. Playing the Winter Gardens for a fortnight.

BILLY. A ballet dancer!

ARCHIE. He was telling me if you drop your hat outside there now, you have to kick it down to the promenade before you can pick it up. (*Pauses quickly, then goes on expertly.*) They're not all coloured, I saw a couple of 'em on the bus on the way home yesterday. They were talking together all the way, everybody listening. I just got up to press the bell, and a woman shouted out, "I lost two boys in the war for the likes of you!" I thought she meant me for a moment, so I turned round, and there she was, beating them with her umbrella like crazy.

BILLY. Don't like to see a man dancing like that.

ARCHIE. I was in a show with a couple of male dancers once. And wherever we went, on the Monday night some woman used to complain about their tights bulging. Wherever we went. Every Monday night. I'm sure it was the same woman each time. I used to call her the Camp Follower. Now, what are we going to have? Let's see what we've got. (*Rummages in carrier and pockets.*)

BILLY. There's a telegram come for you.

PHOEBE. Don't you think she's looking a bit peeky.

ARCHIE. Looks all right to me. Needs a drink that's all.

BILLY (*beginning to get tired and irritable*). There's a telegram come for you!

ARCHIE. Have you been on the batter, you old gubbins?

BILLY. No, I haven't! I've been sitting here talking to Jean.

ARCHIE. I should go to bed if you're tired.

BILLY. I'm not tired—I could see you out any day!

ARCHIE (*picks up telegram*). You've been giving him that beastly gin. He sounds like a toast-master with D.T.s. One of my creditors. It'll wait. (*Throws it back on the table.*) You'd think they'd know better by this time! I've got some gin, too—and Dubonnet. Old Phoebe likes that, don't you, dear! She thinks she's being awfully U when she drinks that, don't you?

PHOEBE. I like it. It seems to suit me. I can't drink gin on its own—not like he can. (*To* ARCHIE.) What's all this for? Was it—was it all right at the theatre?

ARCHIE. No, it wasn't all right at the theatre. Monday night there were sixty sad little drabs in, and tonight there were about two hundred sad little drabs. If we can open on Monday night at West Hartlepool, it will be by very reluctant agreement of about thirty angry people, but I'm not thinking about that tonight.

PHOEBE. Oh, Archie!

ARCHIE. Go on, have your Dubonnet, dear. Don't get all emotional. Jean, that's yours. Billy, wake up!

BILLY. I am awake!

ARCHIE. Well, stop yelling then. You're like one of those television commercials. There's a drink for you.

BILLY. I don't want a bloody drink.

ARCHIE. You look as though you're going to sing a hymn.

BILLY. I'm tired.

ARCHIE. Well, that's better—have a drink and go to bed.

BILLY. I haven't seen the evening paper yet.

ARCHIE. Well, if you've won the pools, we can read about it in the morning.

BILLY. I don't want to sit here and stagnate, even if you do. I want to know what's going on in the world.

ARCHIE. Yes, you're amazingly well informed. (*To the others.*) He's quite well-read for an ignorant old pro.

BILLY. I'm not an ignorant old pro!

ARCHIE. Yes, you are; now don't argue and drink up. I'm having a celebration.

BILLY. Celebration! What have you got to celebrate about!

ARCHIE. Oh dear.

BILLY (*stands up*). You haven't got a thing you can call your own. And as sure as God made little apples, I'll lay a sovereign to a penny piece, you'll end up in the bankruptcy court again before Christmas, and you'll be lucky if you don't land up in jail as well.

PHOEBE. Get 'im to go to bed, Archie. He's over-tired.

BILLY. I'm not over-tired. I don't relish the idea of another jail-bird in the family.

PHOEBE. Be quiet, Dad. You've had too much to drink.

BILLY. I could drink you lot under the table.

ARCHIE. Oh dear, he's getting religious now.

BILLY. I used to have half a bottle of three-star brandy for breakfast—

ARCHIE. And a pound of steak and a couple of chorus girls. He'll tell you the whole story at the drop of a hat.

BILLY (*in rage*). I leave chorus girls to *you*!

ARCHIE. Nothing like slicing yourself off a nice piece of bacon.

BILLY. I know what you mean.

ARCHIE. Don't get excited, Father. You'll wake the Poles up.

BILLY. Don't talk to me about that bunch of greasy tom-cats! One Britisher could always take on half a dozen of that kind. Or used to. Doesn't look like it now.

ARCHIE. Well, never mind, don't spoil the party—

BILLY. I pay my way, which is more than you've ever done. And I'll tell you that I was educated at one of the finest schools in England.

ARCHIE. It produced one Field Marshal with strong Fascist tendencies, one Catholic poet who went bonkers and Archie Rice.

BILLY. D'you know what James Agate said about me?

ARCHIE. Oh yes—that you and Mrs. Pat Campbell were his favourite female impersonators.

BILLY. You know bloody well what he said.

>   (ARCHIE *knows by long experience how far he can go and he manages gently to turn the situation.*)

ARCHIE. We all know what he said, and every word of it was true.

>   (BILLY *glares at him and grabs his glass.*)

Well, as I was saying, before my ignorant old father interrupted—

BILLY. There's nothing to be ashamed of in being an old pro. It's more than you'll ever be. You don't know the meaning of the word!

PHOEBE. Oh, go to bed, Dad—you're getting silly now.

BILLY. You had to have personality to be a comedian then. You had to *really be somebody!*

ARCHIE. The reason for this little celebration is that tomorrow—oh, it's today now—today is my twentieth anniversary.

PHOEBE. Twentieth anniversary? Anniversary of what?

ARCHIE. The twentieth anniversary of my not paying income tax. The last time I paid income tax was in 19—. (*According to date.*)

BILLY. They'll get you all right, they always get you in the end. You see!

ARCHIE. All right, love, you can sing us a hymn later. I think that is a very significant achievement, and I deserve some kind of tribute for it. (*To* JEAN.) Don't you think your old man deserves a tribute?

JEAN. I was just wondering how you came to pay income tax in 19—. (*According to date.*)

ARCHIE. Bad luck, that's all. I was trapped in hospital with a double hernia. Very nasty it was, too. Terribly complicated. I even thought all my plans for the future were going to be finished at one point. Anyway, that's another story. I'll tell you some time. I was lying there on my back, wondering whether draught Bass on its own was enough to make life worth living, when two men in bowlers and rain-coats sprang at me from behind the screens. That was Archie's one downfall. Could have happened to anyone. I think the ward-sister must have tipped them off. She used to tell me she was very spiritual, so she probably did. I'd gone legit. for a while just then, and I'd been in *The Tale of Two Cities.* When I told her she said, "Oh, yes, I think I've heard of that—" (*To* BILLY.) She was an

Irish lady. "—A Tale of Two Cities—isn't it about Sodom and Gomorrah?"

(JEAN *smiles.* BILLY *and* PHOEBE *are no longer listening.*)

A lady in the pit thought that was quite funny tonight.

PHOEBE. Jean's had an upset with Graham.

ARCHIE. Have you? Oh, I'm sorry. I should have asked, shouldn't I? I'm sorry, dear. I'm afraid I'm a wee bit slewed. (*Looks round.*) I think everyone is. You are.

PHOEBE. She's broken off her engagement.

ARCHIE. Have you really? Well, I should have thought engagements were a bit surburban for intellectuals like you, anyway. *You'll* be getting a motor-cycle and side-car next.

PHOEBE. Oh stop poking fun at her, Archie. Be sensible. You can see she's upset.

JEAN. I'm not upset, and I haven't made a decision about anything yet. I just came up because I wanted to see you all, and see how you are. And because I miss you.

PHOEBE. Oh, did you really? That's very sweet of you, dear. I appreciate that, I do really.

ARCHIE. She knows I'm not poking fun at her.

PHOEBE. Oh, I don't know what's going to happen.

JEAN. Never mind about me. You haven't heard from young Mick?

ARCHIE. No, old Mick can look after himself; he's a boy without problems, that one. What's happened with you and Graham?

BILLY. Your daughter went to that Trafalgar Square circus last Sunday, if you please!

ARCHIE. Oh really? Are you one of those who don't like the Prime Minister? I think I've grown rather fond of him. I think it was after he went to the West Indies to get Noel Coward to write a play for him. Still, perhaps only someone of my generation could understand that. Does he bring you out in spots!

PHOEBE. Oh, Christ, I wish I knew what was going to happen to us!

ARCHIE. I feel rather like that about that horrible dog downstairs. It brings me out in a rash every time I look at it. There are three things that do that to me, three things: nuns, clergymen and dogs.

PHOEBE. I don't want to always have to work. I mean you want a bit of life before it's all over. It takes the gilt off if you know you've got to go on and on till they carry you out in a box. It's all right

T.E.—C

for him, he's all right. He's still got his women. While it lasts anyway. But I don't want to end up being lain out by some stranger in
some rotten stinking little street in Gateshead, or West Hartlepool
or another of those dead-or-alive holes!

JEAN. Phoebe, don't upset yourself, please. Let's enjoy ourselves—

PHOEBE. Enjoy myself ! D'you think I don't want to enjoy myself!
I'm just sick of being with down and outs. I'm sick of it, and people
like him. (*She is crying.*)

ARCHIE. I wish women wouldn't cry. I wish they wouldn't. Try and
say something to her, Jean.

JEAN (*going to* PHOEBE). Why don't you?

ARCHIE. I wish I could. I only wish I could.

JEAN (*to* PHOEBE). Come on, dear, would you like to go to bed?

PHOEBE. Yes, I think so, dear, if you don't mind. I think I've over-
done it a bit. Archie knows what I'm like. I never could stand
too much excitement. I think perhaps I got over-excited seeing you.
It was such a nice surprise. And I'm probably worrying about young
Mick underneath. I keep thinking of all that fighting—

ARCHIE. Get some sleep, love, you'll feel better when you wake up.

PHOEBE (*rising*). All right, dear. I'll get along. It's late anyway. Dad
should have been in bed hours ago. He'll be awful tomorrow.
Make him go to bed, Archie, will you?

ARCHIE. I will. (*To* JEAN.) See her up.

PHOEBE (*stopping*). Would you come and say good night to me, Archie?

ARCHIE. Yes. I'm just going to finish my little celebration. It's my
anniversary remember!

PHOEBE (*smiles*). He's funny. (*Exit with* JEAN.)

ARCHIE (*to* BILLY). Want another before you turn in?

BILLY. No, thank you. I have had sufficient.

ARCHIE. Go on, you old gubbins. (*Pours out a drink.*) I know that
expression. That's your hymn look.

BILLY. You think I won't!

ARCHIE. I'm damn sure you will. All right, let's have a good heart
warmer. Then drink up your beer and go to bed.

BILLY. All right. I will. (*He sits upright and sings.*)
Soldiers of the cross, arise!
Gird you with your armour bright;
Mighty are your enemies,
Hard the battle you must fight.

O'er a fruitless fallen world
Raise your banner to the sky.

(JEAN *has come back into the room and* BILLY *is too weary to go on. He starts to move down to his room.*)

BILLY. Good night, Jean. It was good to see you. We'll have a talk tomorrow.

JEAN. Yes, we will. And you're taking me to the club, remember.

BILLY. Good night, son.

ARCHIE. Good night, Dad.

(*Exit* BILLY.)

JEAN. Dad—

ARCHIE. Yes.

JEAN. You're keeping something to yourself.

ARCHIE. You never miss a thing, do you? Observation—is the basis of all art.

JEAN. What is it? I've had a strange sick feeling in my stomach all day. As if something was going to happen. You know the feeling?

ARCHIE. Yes, I know the feeling. Mick's been taken prisoner. He's safe, but he's been taken prisoner. Nobody here seemed to know. It's in the paper, actually. There was no point in breaking it tonight. Tomorrow's soon enough. (*He tears open the telegram.*) They usually get these things before the people who really matter. I knew what this must be. (*He hands it to her and picks up the paper.*) He seems to have been shooting up quite a lot of wogs, doesn't he? There's a picture of your friend here, too, the one who gives you a rash. He's looking rather serious this time. Perhaps he's worrying about young Mick.

JEAN. I think I will have some of that.

(*He pushes her glass towards her.*)

ARCHIE. Well, Mick wouldn't want us to cut the celebration short. We'll drink to Mick, and let's hope to God he manages. Mick and the income tax man. With you it's Prime Ministers, with me it's dogs. Nuns, clergymen and dogs. D'you know the greatest compliment I had paid to me—the greatest compliment I always treasure? I was walking along the front somewhere—I think it was here actually—one day, oh, it must be twenty-five years ago, I was quite a young man. Well, there I was walking along the front, to meet what I think we used to call a piece of crackling. Or perhaps it was a bit of fluff. I can't remember. Anyway, I know I enjoyed it afterwards. But the point is I was walking along the front, all on my own, minding my own business (*Pause.*) and two nuns came towards me— (*Pause.*) two nuns—

(*He trails off, looking very tired and old. He looks across at* JEAN *and pushes the bottle at her.*)

Talk to me.

CURTAIN
INTERMISSION

NUMBER SIX

BILLY, PHOEBE, JEAN, ARCHIE *and* FRANK. PHOEBE *is flushed with drink. Only the first three are on stage.*

BILLY. I knew they couldn't keep him. They wouldn't dare.

PHOEBE. Home in a couple of days—I just can't believe it.

BILLY. They wouldn't dare, not even nowadays—grubby lot of rogues they are. I remember 'em from before the war. I was with that show, you remember, Phoebe?

PHOEBE. Well, what would they want to keep a boy like that for? That's what I kept asking myself. Can't do them any good. It couldn't do them any good, could it?

BILLY. Grubby lot of rogues. I was a guest at the Ambassadors', you know. Gave me a box of Romeo and Juliet cigars.

JEAN (*surrounded by pile of newspapers*). Well, the name of Rice is famous once again.

BILLY. This long they were. Haven't had a cigar like that for years.

PHOEBE. He likes a cigar. I buy those cheroots sometimes. They're only cheap things, but he doesn't mind them, does he?

BILLY. Course I don't mind them. Jeannie gave me some, didn't she? What's the matter with you?

PHOEBE. Oh yes, I was forgetting.

BILLY. Got a mind like a bloody sieve.

PHOEBE. I was always a dunce at school. I keep thinking of Archie. I'm so afraid that he's going to be disappointed. That everything will go wrong, and they won't let him go, after all.

BILLY. Pardon me, Phoebe, but you do talk the most almighty rubbish I've ever had to sit and listen to.

JEAN. They've given a formal undertaking.

BILLY. Formal undertaking, my backside—if I thought that boy's future depended on their "formal undertaking" we could say "thank you very much and good night".

PHOEBE (*paper in her lap*). They've got an aeroplane standing by all ready to rush him home.

BILLY. "Formal undertaking"—proper politician's words they are. They'd mean damn all if they were said by one of ours.

JEAN (*reading*). "Bring him home"—in a matter of a few hours Sergeant Rice should be speeding homewards in a specially allocated aircraft standing by.

BILLY. They know damn well they daren't do anything else.

JEAN. They're going to have themselves a hero, you can see that—

BILLY. Any one of us would have done the same thing. There's nothing wrong with any of us, never has been. You can't all get to the top. You can't make your own luck. Me, I was always lucky, always was. Mind you, I was good, too. That Ambassador, Sir Somebody Pearson his name was, charming, absolutely, the real best type, absolutely the best type: he told me I was his favourite artist—barring George Robey.

PHOEBE. What good would it do them, hanging on to a kid? That's all he is.

JEAN. This one says—

BILLY. He's lucky. I was always lucky. Never had a day's illness in my life. I was never off, not once. You knew that, didn't you? Yes, of course, you'd know that.

JEAN (*reading*). "Lieut. Pearson, of Leicester, who had been with Sergeant Rice until a few minutes before he was captured, said he must have killed at least seven of the attackers—"

BILLY. Was that Pearson, you said?

JEAN. "—before he was overwhelmed. 'He must have run out of ammunition,' said Pearson. 'Young Rice wasn't the type to give up'."

(*Pause.*)

PHOEBE. I don't want *him* to be disappointed, that's all. On top of everything else. He's had enough of disappointments. I don't think he ever really gets used to them.

BILLY. You see, a couple of days, and he'll be sitting down here talking about it.

PHOEBE. I remember once my Mum promised to take us kids to the pantomime (*She pronounces it "pantermime".*) and then something

happened, she couldn't take us. I don't know what it was, she
didn't have the money, I expect. You could sit up in the gallery then
for sixpence. But I expect Dad had to have it for something. I
expect that's what happened anyway. Poor old Mum—she took us
later, but it didn't seem the same to me. I was too disappointed. I'd
been thinking about that pantomime for weeks. You shouldn't
build things up. You're always disappointed really. That's Archie's
trouble. He always builds everything up. And it never turns out.

BILLY. He's a fool.

PHOEBE. He's too good for them, that's his trouble. People don't
appreciate you properly. Let's finish this up, shall we? Archie'll
bring some more in with him when he comes.

BILLY. It's all over, finished. I told him years ago. But he won't
listen. He won't listen to anybody.

PHOEBE. You can't help giving Archie his own way. Not really.
No, all they're out for is a cheap thrill. (*To* JEAN.) Come on, have
half of this with me. We've all got to—what's the word?

BILLY. I dunno what you're talking about.

JEAN. Compromise?

PHOEBE. She knows what I mean. That's right, dear. You keep on
and on, try your best, and then a time comes when you can't go on
any longer. It's not giving in—or I suppose it is. It's just being sensible. (*To* JEAN.) Has he said anything to you?

JEAN. What about?

PHOEBE. Oh, about anything. He never tells me anything now, he
just tells me not to worry, and says nothing. Frank told me the
company only got half salary on Saturday night, and he thinks these
scenery people must have caught up with him because—

BILLY. He said he'd bring me back some cigarettes. I could have got
them myself by this time. I suppose he's in that Rockliffe.

PHOEBE. Whenever there's a ring at the door, I daren't answer it, in
case it's a policeman standing there with another summons.

JEAN (*offering cigarettes to* BILLY). Have one of these.

BILLY. That bloody meat-market.

PHOEBE. It's not a nice feeling when you can't go and answer the
door.

BILLY. There'll be a policeman at the door all right—

PHOEBE (*weary, not peevish*). Oh don't keep interrupting while I'm
talking to Jean.

BILLY (*to* JEAN, *politely*). Thank you, my dear. (*Picks up his newspaper.*)

PHOEBE. I've upset him now.

JEAN. No you haven't. He's just reading, aren't you, Grandad?

BILLY. Um?

PHOEBE. Oh well, it's no good worrying. Is it? It says in the papers Mick's coming home, and they ought to know about these things, and that's all that really matters. Have a drop of this, dear.

BILLY. No, thank you.

PHOEBE (*to* JEAN). Pour him out a glass. There's one over there. Oh, Dad, he exaggerates everything, don't you? He exaggerates everything, but he's right, you know. He's right about Archie. He hasn't got an enemy in the world who's done him the harm he's done himself.

JEAN. There you are, Grandad.

BILLY. Thank you, Jean. I'll have it later.

JEAN. Don't have it later. Have it now. This is the time to celebrate. Come on then. Let's drink to Mick.

PHOEBE. Yes, we mustn't sit here, getting morbid. We're a bit short on the drink, aren't we? I hope Archie won't be long in that place.

JEAN. Frank's gone with him. He won't be long.

PHOEBE. Oh Frank'll see he doesn't get home too late. Frank's a sensible boy—sometimes he is, anyway. (*To* JEAN.) I think you're the only really sensible one of us lot.

JEAN. Grandad doesn't think so, do you?

BILLY. She's just as bloody daft as the rest of you.

PHOEBE. He's a fool to himself. Always some big idea he's got to make money. A while back it was female impersonators. We were going to make a packet. That's what Archie said, anyway. Somebody else was supposed to have played to three thousand odd a week at Brighton with one of those shows, and it was the same all over. But by the time Archie got started with it it had all petered out. People didn't want it any more. They soon get tired, they want something different, and you can't blame 'em. There's always the nudes, of course, but Archie could never get the top-liners to work for him. Now it's rock and roll. Oh well. It's like the women. They get tired of him. They come back here a few times, and that's that—

BILLY. Why don't you hold your bloody noise!

PHOEBE. He doesn't like me talking about it. As if she didn't know what's been going on all this time.

BILLY. Well, there's no reason to talk about it.

PHOEBE. She's not soft, are you, dear?

BILLY. I don't want to hear about it, and I shouldn't think she does.

PHOEBE. All right, all right.

BILLY. She's used to being with people who know how to behave. She doesn't want to hear about your troubles.

PHOEBE. No, of course she doesn't.

BILLY. Well then—the trouble with you people is you don't know how to carry on properly, that's your trouble. Give the girl a chance, she's got her own life to lead.

PHOEBE. I was only telling her—

BILLY. And I'm telling you—don't! There's nothing *you* can tell her. So hold your noise—

JEAN. Grandad, please—

BILLY. Why don't you go back to London to your friends?

JEAN. Don't let's argue—

BILLY. We're no good to you—

JEAN. I don't think I want to go back to London—

PHOEBE. I was only talking to her about Archie. You don't want to leave, do you, dear?

JEAN. Of course I don't.

PHOEBE. I was just saying, in the course of ordinary conversation, that Archie wasn't very lucky, that's all.

JEAN. Here— (*She has put a small bottle of gin on the table.*)

PHOEBE. And if I mention the women, it was just because it's been the same thing with them. It's never bothered me, that, so much. It never meant a great deal to me, not even when I was young. Still, I suppose men are different. It's more important to them. Oh, look what she's done!

JEAN. I thought I'd better get some in, in case Dad was late.

BILLY. What do you think you're supposed to be—a millionairess?

JEAN. But you're not to have any, till you've had something to eat first, you've had nothing but tea and cigarettes for days.

PHOEBE. I couldn't eat anything, dear. Honestly.

JEAN. I'll get it for you.

PHOEBE. No, I couldn't. I couldn't—hold it down.

JEAN (*moving*). I'm not going to argue—

PHOEBE. Jean, I've asked you—I can't! I don't want it!

JEAN. But people have got to eat, dear. If you don't have something—

THE ENTERTAINER

PHOEBE (*laughing slightly*). People have to eat, she says. That's a good one!

JEAN. You can't carry on, dear.

(BILLY *gets up humming "Rock of Ages" and goes off* L.)

PHOEBE. People have to eat, she says. D'you hear that? Where's he got to?

JEAN. He's just gone into the kitchen.

PHOEBE. That's not all they have to do. They have to do a whole lot of things, a lot of things you don't even know about, and it's nothing to do with being educated and all that. Why should you know about it?

JEAN. I know, love. Things have been tough. But be sensible, you've got to keep on.

PHOEBE. Don't tell me to be sensible, Jean.

JEAN. I'm sorry, dear. I didn't mean it like that—

PHOEBE. Don't tell me to be sensible! You're a sweet girl, Jean, and I'm very fond of you. But you're not even my own daughter. I wouldn't take that from Mick or Frank, and they're my own.

JEAN. All right, forget it. We'll forget it. We haven't had our drink to Mick yet.

PHOEBE. Don't—don't presume too much.

JEAN. Phoebe, please—I just—

PHOEBE. Don't presume too much. What's he doing out there?

JEAN. He's probably getting him something to eat, I expect.

PHOEBE. I don't want him messing about out there. He knows I don't like him going out there. He leaves everything in such a mess.

JEAN. Here, have this.

PHOEBE. Why doesn't Archie come back? You'd think he'd come back here and celebrate after hearing his son is safe and on his way home. I don't know—you people—

JEAN. Come along, Phoebe, don't let's have a row. And over nothing —it's silly.

PHOEBE. It's not silly. Anyway, who said we're having a row? All I said was I wasn't hungry, and you start getting at me.

JEAN. I wasn't getting at you.

PHOEBE. You people—you're all alike.

JEAN. Believe me, Phoebe, I wasn't—

PHOEBE. I can't eat because I feel sick.

JEAN. Well, all right then.

PHOEBE. You don't know what it's like. You don't know what it's like because we tried to do our best by you. Oh, Archie tried to do his best by you, even if it didn't add up to very much. Not that you weren't a good girl, you worked hard. You deserved it, you've always tried, and you've got what it takes. And that's more than any of us have got, my dear. You're the only one of us who has. You and young Mick. And the old man of course. He had it. Not that it's any use to him now. He's just a has-been, I suppose. Still, it's better to be a has-been than a never-was. His other son's the same—old Bill. Archie's brother. Not that you'd think he was. Now he's really a big pot. He's really a big pot. There's no flies on brother Bill.

JEAN (*trying to turn the conversation*). He's a barrister—that's why you like him so much. He's like that actor on the pictures who's always in a wig and gown in every other—

PHOEBE. I like him because he's a gentleman. He's different from your father, even if they did go to the same posh school and all that. I like him because of the way he treats me. He talks to me beautifully, the way he calls me "Phoebe". You should hear the way he calls me "Phoebe".

JEAN. I only saw him a couple of times.

PHOEBE. Well, of course you did. He didn't approve of the way Archie carried on. He never did. Sometimes in the early days, he'd come and see us. He always slipped a couple of fivers in my hand before he left, and he'd just say "Not a word to Archie now". I just never used to know what to say to him. We'd always be living in some bloody digs somewhere, and I didn't like him coming. I'd feel awful. He could never bring his wife, and I never knew what to say. Then he and Archie would always have a row over something Archie had been doing. Either he'd lost money, or he was out of work. I remember he came once, and Archie and me didn't have a bean. We'd been living on penny pieces of bacon from the butchers, and what we got then from the Tribunal. (*She pronounces it "Tribbunel".*) You and the boys were staying with the Old Man then. Archie wouldn't take money from his Dad, then—perhaps it was professional jealousy, I don't know. Anyway, Bill heard that Archie was in trouble again—I don't remember what it was. But it was something serious this time, I think. Oh, he tried to pass a dud cheque and he'd picked the wrong person or something. That wasn't like Archie, I must admit, because he never did anything really dishonest like that, whatever else he might have done. He must have been drunk. Anyway, old Bill came over—we were living at Brixton at that time, and the kids in the street made a terrible mess of his car. They didn't see many cars in that street except when it was the doctor. Not that he said a word about it. When we went to the door, and I saw what they'd done to it, I just stood there, I felt so ashamed, and I burst out crying. He patted my arm in that way of his and he just said: "I'm so sorry, Phoebe. I really am. I'm afraid it's always going to be like this". Well, he got Archie out of whatever it was, and that was that. It wasn't the money, or his helping Archie—although I was grateful for that, of course. It was the way he spoke to me in that quiet gentlemanly way, and the way he patted my arm.

JEAN. Yes, I can see him doing it.

PHOEBE. What do you mean—what do you mean by that remark?

JEAN. Oh nothing, dear. Let's not talk about it—

PHOEBE. What do you mean by that remark?

JEAN. Oh, it's just that I can see brother Bill patting your arm, slipping that ten pounds in your hand, and then driving off to have dinner at his club. That's all, Phoebe. Now let's not talk about it any more.

PHOEBE. You mean he was just sorry for me, don't you?

JEAN. No, I don't.

PHOEBE. Come on, say it—you mean he was just sorry for me, don't you?

JEAN. I didn't say that and I didn't mean that. Now come on—
    (*Enter* ARCHIE *with* FRANK. FRANK *is a pale, shy boy about nineteen. He has allowed himself to slip into the role of* ARCHIE'S *"feed" because this seems to be a warm, reasonable relationship substitute that suits them both. He is impulsive, full of affection that spills over easily. He is young, and will probably remain so.*)

PHOEBE. I want to know what you meant.

ARCHIE. My dear, nobody can tell you what they mean. You ought to know that by now.

PHOEBE. Shut up a minute, Archie, I'm talking to Jean. She knows what I mean. You know what I meant, don't you?

ARCHIE. Do you know what she means? I wish to God I did. (*To* FRANK.) I can see we should have stayed.

PHOEBE. Shall I tell you something?

JEAN. Phoebe, what are you doing?

PHOEBE. Shall I?

JEAN. It's just that I know exactly how Uncle Bill patted your arm—
just in the same way as he'd wait on the men at Christmas when he
was in the army. So democratic, so charming and so English.

ARCHIE. Oh, Bill's all right. Just doesn't understand people like us,
that's all. And what's more he doesn't want to. Can't blame him
really.

PHOEBE (to JEAN). You don't like him, do you? I knew you didn't
like him.

ARCHIE. Like now. Oh, brother Bill wouldn't understand all this at
all. He'd be frightfully embarrassed, wouldn't he? Give us over
that carrier, Frankie love.

PHOEBE. You can't afford not to like him. You owe him too much.

ARCHIE. Sounds a pretty good reason for not liking anyone, I should say.

PHOEBE. He's something you'll never be.

ARCHIE. And I'm something he'll never be—good old Bill. He may
have lots of money, but he's not a bad sort. Do you know that my
brother, Bill, has had one wife, no love affair, he's got three, charming, gifted children? Two of them took honours degrees at Cambridge, and all of them have made what these people call highly
successful marriages.

FRANK. What on earth's everybody talking about? Hullo Jean, love.
I thought we were going to have a party.

(He throws his arms round her and kisses her.)

ARCHIE. It's perfectly true. I read it in the Telegraph today. I got
bored reading about young Mick, and there, tucked away in the
middle—

JEAN (eagerly). Don't tell me you read—

ARCHIE. Of course, I read it. How else would I know whether my
relations were getting married, or dying, or having babies. As I was
saying—

FRANK. Before you were so rudely interrupted.

(Kissing JEAN affectionately once again.)

ARCHIE. Yes, before that. Young Sonia is getting married.

JEAN. Who to?

ARCHIE. Oh, the son of some industrialist, Captain Charlie Double-
back-Action hyphen-breech loading Gore of Elm Lodge, Shrewkesbury, Glos. Where are all the glasses, for God's sake? Good ole
Bill—he's got everything he wants now, including Captain Charlie
Double-back-Action Gore.

PHOEBE. Archie, I'm talking to Jean.

ARCHIE. Yes, I thought that's what you were doing. I sized the situation up in a flash.

PHOEBE. Oh, it's easy for people like you to make fun. I left school when I was twelve years old.

ARCHIE. Christ, if she tells me that once more I shall get up on the roof, drunk as I am, I shall get up on the roof and scream. I've never done that before.

PHOEBE. You had to pay sixpence a week then.

FRANK. Leave her alone, you old bastard. Come on, Mum, we're going to have a party.

PHOEBE. I'm talking to Jean.

ARCHIE. Yes, we were in on that. Why don't we all talk to Jean? We don't see much of her. Frank, talk to Jean.

FRANK. Dad—

> (*He nods towards* PHOEBE, *distressed to see her like this, but* ARCHIE, *who has come in prepared to be gay, is tired and has begun to give up the situation.*)

ARCHIE. Let's have a drink first. If I'm going to be either very diplomatic, or very tactful, I must have plenty to drink first.

PHOEBE. We had to pay sixpence a week, and most weeks my mother couldn't find it—

ARCHIE. This is a welfare state, my darling heart. Nobody wants, and nobody goes without, all are provided for.

PHOEBE. I was out scrubbing a dining hall for—

ARCHIE. Everybody's all right. Young Mick's all right. Bill's all right. Why, he never even got himself jailed by a lot of wogs. Frank's all right—he won't be stoking boilers much longer, will you boy?

FRANK. I wish you'd both shut up.

ARCHIE. Jean's all right. She'll make it up with Graham, and forget about silly old Trafalgar Square, and Prime Ministers who look like dogs downstairs. Here you are, dear. (*Offers drink to* PHOEBE.)

PHOEBE. You don't understand—

ARCHIE. Phoebe scrubbed a dining hall floor for five hundred kids when she was twelve years old, didn't you?

PHOEBE. Oh—

ARCHIE. Didn't you? Have you any idea, any of you, have you any idea how often she's told me about those five hundred kids and that dining hall?

FRANK. Oh, shut up.

ARCHIE. Yes, son, I'll shut up. Pass this to Jean. She looks as though she can use it.

JEAN. I can.

FRANK. You've been away too long. Every night is party night.

ARCHIE. And do you know why? Do you know why? Because we're dead beat and down and outs. We're drunks, maniacs, we're crazy, we're bonkers, the whole flaming bunch of us. Why, we have problems that nobody's ever heard of, we're characters out of something that nobody believes in. We're something that people make jokes about, because we're so remote from the rest of ordinary everyday, human experience. But we're not really funny. We're too boring. Simply because we're not like anybody who ever lived. We don't get on with anything. We don't ever succeed in anything. We're a *nuisance,* we do nothing but make a God almighty fuss about anything we ever do. All the time we're trying to draw someone's attention to our nasty, sordid, unlikely little problems— like that poor, pathetic old thing there. Look at her. What has she got to do with people like you? People of intellect and sophistication. She's very drunk, and just now her muzzy, under-developed, untrained mind is racing because her blood stream is full of alcohol I can't afford to give her, and she's going to force us to listen to all sorts of dreary embarrassing things we've all heard a hundred times before. She's getting old, and she's worried about who's going to keep her when she can't work any longer. She's afraid of ending up in a long box in somebody else's front room in Gateshead, or was it West Hartlepool?

PHOEBE. What's he talking about?

ARCHIE. She's going to tell you that old brother Bill paid for all your education. That's what she wants to tell you, Jean. That scholarship didn't pay for the things that really mattered, you know. The books, the fares, the clothes, and all the rest of it. Bill paid for that. For all of you. Frank knows that, don't you, Frank? I'm sorry, Phoebe. I've killed your story. Old Archie could always kill anybody's punch line if he wanted.

PHOEBE. She doesn't know about Mick. I know she doesn't.

ARCHIE. She'll find out. We always find these things out in time. (*To* FRANK *and* JEAN.) She's tired and she's getting old. She's tired, and she's tired of me. Nobody ever gave her two pennyworth of equipment except her own pretty unimpressive self to give anything else to the rest of the world. All it's given her is me, and my God she's tired of that! Aren't you, my old darling? You're tired of that, aren't you?

PHOEBE (*fiercely*). I tried to make something of myself. I tried, I really did try. I was nothing much to look at, but what I was I made myself. I was a plain kid—no, I wasn't. I wasn't even plain. I was the ugliest bloody kid you ever saw in your life. You've never seen anyone as ugly as I was. But I made something of myself. I did try to do something. I made him want me, anyway.

FRANK. Everyone shouts! Please, somebody speak quietly, just for once. Those bloody Poles will be up here in a minute. Let's have a row. It looks as if we're going to have one anyway. But please can we have a *quiet* row!

ARCHIE. It was a long time ago. They know it was a long time ago. (*To* FRANK.) I wish you'd stop yelling, I can't hear myself shout. Sing one of your songs, there's a good boy. Where's the old man?

JEAN. He's in the kitchen.

ARCHIE. Billy! Come out of there! Who's he got in there? Something you picked up in the Cambridge! Have you ever had it on a kitchen table? Like a piece of meat on a slab. Slicing pieces of bacon. Don't you wish you were back with old Graham? (*To* JEAN.)

PHOEBE. Frank, he's going to bring up one of those women, isn't he? In here, isn't he?

ARCHIE. Leave her alone, son.

PHOEBE. Do you think I don't lie awake upstairs, and hear it going on?

ARCHIE. Of course they know. They know what sort of a bastard I am, love. I think they know almost as well as you do. Well, almost as well. She'll be all right, won't you, love? Where's the old man? (*To* FRANK *and* JEAN.) Now don't pretend you're not used to it.

(BILLY *appears*, L.)

There you are, you old has-been! Have you brought us a slice of bacon in?

BILLY. What's the matter with you lot?

ARCHIE. We're all just waiting for the little yellow van to come—

BILLY. Did you get my cigarettes?

ARCHIE. Except for Jean. There's still hope for her. You wait, you old gubbins, you'll be reading about your granddaughter and Mr.

Graham Thing of Elm Lodge, Shrewkesbury, Glos. Here you are. (*Tosses cigarettes to* BILLY *and gives him a drink.*)

PHOEBE (*to* BILLY). You've been at that cake.

BILLY. What?

PHOEBE. You've been at my cake. You've been at my cake, haven't you?

BILLY (*flushing*). I was hungry—

PHOEBE. That cake was for Mick. It was for Mick, it wasn't for you.

BILLY. I'm sorry—

PHOEBE. I bought it for Mick. It was for when he comes home.

ARCHIE. Well, never mind.

PHOEBE. What do you mean—never mind!

ARCHIE. Mick wouldn't mind.

PHOEBE. Well, I mind. I don't want him in that kitchen. Tell him to keep out of it. It's not much, and it's not mine, but I mind very much. Why couldn't you leave it alone?

BILLY. I just fancied—

PHOEBE. Couldn't you leave it alone? It wasn't for you. What's the matter with you? I feed you, don't I? Don't think you give me all that much money every week, because you don't!

ARCHIE. Phoebe, forget it!

PHOEBE. I don't forget, I don't forget anything. I don't forget anything even if you do.

ARCHIE. We'll buy another one.

PHOEBE. Oh, you'll buy another one! You're so rich! You're such a great big success! What's a little cake—we'll order a dozen of 'em! I bought that cake, and it cost me thirty shillings, it was for Mick when he comes back, because I want to give him something, something I know he'll like, after being where he's been, and going through what he has—and now, that bloody *greedy* old pig—that old pig, as if he hadn't had enough of everything already—he has to go and get his great fingers into it!

　　　(*Unable to top this, she bursts into tears.* BILLY *stands, ashamed and deeply hurt by what she has said, even though he vaguely realizes the condition she is in. He puts down the drink he has been holding, and cigarettes.*)

BILLY. Excuse me, Jean.

　　　(*He crosses down to his room and goes out.*)

PHOEBE. Archie, you haven't got anybody coming tonight, have you?

ARCHIE. I suppose he has had more than any of us, and he's enjoyed it.

Good luck to him. All the same, you needn't have done that. No, there's nobody coming.

PHOEBE. Oh, I'm sorry, Archie. Try and forgive me—

ARCHIE. Not that I don't wish there were. But then you know that. Come on, love, pull yourself together. That's what we should have done years ago. Pulled ourselves together. Let's pull ourselves together. (*Sings.*) Let's pull ourselves together, together, together. Let's pull ourselves together, and the happier we shall be!

FRANK. That's right, chaps—remember we're British!

ARCHIE. That's what everybody does. Perfectly simple. I've always known it. That's what my old brother Bill used to tell me. Now let's fill up and be happy. What about old Mick, eh?

FRANK. Yes, what about old Mick? Don't look so glum, Jean. You know what everybody's like.

JEAN. Do I?

ARCHIE. Never mind, there's no reason why she should, as Phoebe would say. We're all a bit slewed, which means that we're a bit more sub-human even than we usually are. (*To* FRANK.) Isn't that right, you great weedy boiler stoker you! I'll bet the patients in that hospital all freeze to death—he must be saving the National Health thousands.

FRANK (*to* PHOEBE). Feel all right now?

PHOEBE. Perhaps Jean doesn't want to have a drink, and do you know why?

ARCHIE. No, why?

PHOEBE. Because I don't think she even likes him. I don't think she likes Mick.

ARCHIE. There's no reason why she should. But that won't stop her. Or me. Frank, go in and talk to the old man, and get him to come back. We'll try to be a little normal just for once, and pretend we're a happy, respectable, decent family. For Mick's sake. You know, I really think that's what he'd like somehow. I'm sure he thinks we're rather dreadful. Worse than the wogs really. Don't worry, Jean, you won't have to put up with this kind of thing for long— any more than Mick. And this is Mick's party. Phoebe, let's see you do your dance. (*This is thrown off in the usual casual, studied* ARCHIE *manner.*) She dances jolly well, don't you, you poor old thing? I wonder if she'll make me cry tonight. We'll see. We'll see. Frank, sing us your song.

T.E.—D

JEAN. I don't even know what I'm feeling. I don't even know if I do at all.

ARCHIE. Never mind, dear. I didn't know that for years, either. You're a long time dead, Mrs. Murphy, let's make it a party. Mick the soldier's coming back, let's just whoop it up.

CURTAIN

NUMBER SEVEN

Music. ARCHIE *enters, his face held open by a grin, and dead behind the eyes. Just now and then, for a second or two, he gives the tiniest indication that he is almost surprised to find himself where he is.*

ARCHIE. Here, here! Here, I've just seen a man with a lemon stuck in his ear! A lemon stuck in his ear! So I went up to him, I said: "What are you doing with that lemon stuck in your ear?" and he says: "Well, you know that man with a hearing aid—well I'm the man with the lemonade". Thank you for that burst of heavy breathing. You should have heard what James Agate said about *me!* (*Back again.*) But I have a go, lady, don't I? I 'ave a go. I do. You think I am, don't you? Well, I'm not. But *he* is! Here, here! Did I tell you about the wife? Did I? The wife—my wife. She's gone in for this modelling lark. You know—in these posh magazines! My wife—not only is she stupid, not only is she stupid, but she's cold as well. Oh yes, cold. She may look sweet, but she's a very cold woman, my wife. Very cold. Cold and stupid. She's what they call a moron, glacee. Don't clap too hard—it's a very old building. I'm not kidding, I'm not! Well, I 'ave a go, don't I? I do—I 'ave a go. Look at me—it's all real, you know. Me—all real, nothing shoddy. You don't think I'm real, do you? Well, I'm not. (*Stumbling.*) I'm not going to deprive you of the treat I know you've all been waiting for. Yes, I'm going to sing to you. I'm going to sing to you a little song, a little song written by myself. I haven't recorded it, so if you like it you tell 'em. They won't listen, but you tell 'em. A little song called "My girl's always short of breath, but she don't mind a good blow through".

(He sings.)

Now I'm just an ordinary bloke
The same as you out there.
Not mad for women, not a soak,
I never really care.
Thank God I'm normal, normal, normal
So thank God I'm normal,
I'm just like the rest of you chaps.

Thank God I'm normal,
I'm just like the rest of you chaps,
Decent and full of good sense,
I'm not one of these extremist chaps,
For I'm sure you'll agree,
That a fellow like me
Is the salt of our dear old country,
    of our dear old country.

(Bang on appropriate lighting. Speaking.)

But when our heritage is threatened
At home or across the sea.

(Lower Union Flag.)

It's chaps like us—yes, you and me,
Who'll march again to victory.
Some people say we're finished,
Some people say we're done.
But if we all stand

    *(Spotlight behind gauze reveals a nude in Britannia's helmet and
    holding a bulldog and trident.)*

By this dear old land,
The battle will be won.

Thank God we're normal, normal, normal.
So thank God we're normal.
We are the country's flower,
And when the great call comes,
Someone will gaze down on us,
And say: They made no fuss—
For this was their finest shower.

Yes, this was their finest shower!
And thank God we're normal, normal, normal,
Yes thank God we're normal,
Yes, this was our finest shower!
                    (*Exit.*)

NUMBER EIGHT

ARCHIE, FRANK, PHOEBE, BILLY *and* JEAN.

ARCHIE. She'd steal your knickers and sell 'em for dusters.

FRANK. Who?

ARCHIE. Mrs. Roberts, Number Seven Claypit Lane, always used to say that.

FRANK. Who are you talking about, you bloody, right-wing old poup?

ARCHIE. I'm talking about that blonde bitch in the Cambridge, the one who's always upsetting your Grandad. And don't call me a right-wing old poup.

PHOEBE. I remember Mrs. Roberts. She was very nice to us.

ARCHIE. I may be an old poup, but I'm not right-wing.

FRANK. That's strictly for cigar smokers like Grandad. (*Dancing.*) "Oh, the end of me old cigar, cigar, the end of me old cigar; I turned 'em round and touched 'em up with the end of me old cigar! The end of me old cigar, cigar, the end of me old cigar—"

ARCHIE. There was a chap at my school who managed to get himself into the Labour Government, and they always said he was left of centre. Then he went into the House of Lords, and they made him an honourable fishmonger. Well, that just about wraps up the Left of Centre, doesn't it?

FRANK. You know, you don't know what you're talking about.

BILLY. I used to have digs in Claypit Lane—ten shillings a week all-in.

PHOEBE. Frank, I thought you were going to sing.

ARCHIE. If you can dodge all the *clichés* dropping like bats from the ceiling, you might pick up something from me.

FRANK. Well, plenty of others have picked it up from you.

ARCHIE. Just you remember I'm your father.

FRANK. When did you ever remember it?

PHOEBE. Frank! Come on now, be a good boy.

ARCHIE. You want to be more like Jean—

FRANK. She's just not used to us any more. Are you, love? Are you all right?

(*Puts his arm round her.*)

JEAN. I'm all right.

FRANK. Are you really? Bet you'd forgotten what this was like, didn't you?

PHOEBE. Course she hadn't forgotten. She doesn't forget as easy as that, do you, dear?

JEAN. No—I don't think so.

FRANK (*to* PHOEBE). You're feeling better?

PHOEBE. Yes, thank you, dear. Come over here and give me a kiss. (*He does so.*) He's a good boy to me, aren't you, dear? Even when I act a bit daft. We all act a bit daft sometimes, I suppose.

ARCHIE. Except Jean—

JEAN. Will you please stop trying to make me feel as if I were from another planet or something?

PHOEBE. Archie's just pulling your leg, aren't you, Archie? I didn't have my Beecham's Pills yesterday. D'you know, my mother never had a doctor in her life—except when we were born, of course—and all she ever took was two pennorth of Beecham's, peroxide, and Dutch drops?

JEAN. Peroxide?

FRANK. She used to drink it like Guinness.

PHOEBE. Well, she lived to be ninety-three and never cost the Government a penny. (*To* BILLY.) All right?

BILLY. Yes, thank you, Phoebe.

PHOEBE (*to* ARCHIE). Put something in his glass, Archie. It's nearly empty.

BILLY. I was just trying to remember the name of the woman.

PHOEBE. What woman?

BILLY. The one in Claypit Lane. She used to give us bacon every morning for breakfast, and she'd melt cheese over it. First time I'd ever had it.

PHOEBE. Don't like anything like that much. Here, did you—pardon my interruption but I just remembered it—did you see that picture of the Duchess of Porth's daughter in the paper today?

FRANK. Should we?

PHOEBE. I wouldn't have seen it. I was only really reading about Mick, of course, but I couldn't help noticing it. She looked so fascinating. Did you see it, Archie?

ARCHIE. Oh yes. She was next to Captain Breech-Loading Gore.

PHOEBE. Didn't you think she looked magnificent?

ARCHIE. I thought she looked like Dad's barmaid in the Cambridge.

FRANK. Yes—in drag.

PHOEBE. Frank!

ARCHIE (*quickly*). Phoebe's very keen on the Duchess of Porth, aren't you, love? She says she thinks she's natural.

PHOEBE. I suppose it's a bit silly, but I've always taken an interest in her. Oh, ever since she was quite young. I feel she must be very nice somehow. (*Pause. To* ARCHIE.) Is he all right? (*Nodding to* BILLY.)

ARCHIE. He's all right. You're all right, aren't you? He's thinking about that landlady in Claypit Lane. You know, that barmaid in the Cambridge reminds me of a bloke— (*To* JEAN.) this'll interest you because it's Prime Ministers and Dogs—he was Irish, he did a trampoline act and they called him "Lady Rosie Bothways". Actually, he was a decent sort of a lad. He gave it all up later and went into Public Relations or something. Well, Rosie knew more dirty words than you'll hear in any place on any Saturday night. He could go on for ten minutes without pausing for breath, or repeating himself once. He was an artist. But to Rosie the most deadly four-letter word in the English—or any other—language, was Tory. He'd apply it to anything, provided he thought it was really bad enough.

BILLY. I'll bet he was bloody Irish.

ARCHIE. I've just said so. Do try and listen.

PHOEBE. I thought Frank was going to sing.

ARCHIE. If you gave him a plate of badly cooked chips, he'd hold 'em up and say: "What are these no-good, blank, blank, stinking, Tory chips?"

FRANK. You've told that story before.

ARCHIE. I'll bodge you in a minute.

FRANK. I'll bodge *you* in a minute. It's not even a very good story.

ARCHIE. When you learn to tell a story as well as I do, you'll be all right—

FRANK. I'll never look *old* enough, to tell your stories.

ARCHIE. I think you'd better sing, don't you?

FRANK. All right, all right, I will. I'll sing for Jean, because she hasn't heard me. I'm going to sing one of Billy's. It's British—

BILLY. What's that? What song?

FRANK. And very religious.

BILLY. What song's he singing?

FRANK. So there's something in it for you all.

(*He sings and dances.*)

*When you've shouted "Rule Britannia,"
When you've sung "God Save the Queen,"
When you've finished killing Kruger with your mouth,
Will you kindly drop a shilling in my little tambourine
For a gentleman in khaki ordered South?
He's an absent-minded beggar, and his weaknesses are great—
But we and Paul must take him as we find him—
He is out on active service, wiping something off a slate—
And he's left a lot of little things behind him!
Cook's son, duke's son, son of a belted Earl—
Fifty thousand horse and foot going to Table Bay.
Each of 'em doing his country's work
(And who's to look after their things?)
Pass the hat for your credit's sake, and pay—pay—pay!

BILLY. Pass the hat for your credit's sake, and pay, pay, pay.

ARCHIE. Not bad for an amateur.

BILLY. Last time I sang that was in a pub, some place in Yorkshire.
If you bought a pint of beer, you could get a plateful of Yorkshire
pudding then, as much as you could eat. All for tuppence.

ARCHIE. Come off it, Dad. Nobody ever gave away stuff like that,
not even when you remember.

BILLY. I tell you you got a plate of Yorkshire pudding—

ARCHIE. You're getting really old.

BILLY. As much as you could eat.

ARCHIE. Your mind's going, Dad. I should sit down.

BILLY. I *am* sitting down.

ARCHIE. Getting feeble.

PHOEBE. Archie—don't tease him.

BILLY. I'm not feeble! I'm not half as bloody feeble as you are—thank
God! (*Suddenly sees them smiling at him.*) Thank God I'm not, that's
all. You think you can have it over me all right. Give me some
of that!

*This extract from "The Absent Minded Beggar", from *The Definitive Edition of Rudyard
Kipling's Verse*, is reproduced by kind permission of Mrs. George Bambridge.

FRANK. When there isn't a girl about you feel so lonely. When there isn't a girl about you're on your only—

ARCHIE. Be quiet a minute, will you? I'm trying to think. Ah! Yes. Yes. The girl I love is up in the lavatory, the girl I love is looking down on me.

PHOEBE. No, don't do that, Archie. Don't sing it like that! (*To* JEAN *and* FRANK.) He always used to sing that song, didn't you? It was his favourite, I think.

JEAN. You sing it.

PHOEBE. Me—Oh I can't sing. I don't know even if I can remember the words.

FRANK. Go on, love, have a go.

PHOEBE (*to* ARCHIE). Shall I? (*He nods shortly.*) All right, then.
(*She sings.*)
Oh, the boy I love he's up in the gallery
The boy I love is looking down at me.
Where is he?
There is he,
Waving of his handkerchee,
Happy as the robin
That sings on the tree.

JEAN. Thank you, Phoebe. Thank you.

PHOEBE. It sounded bloody awful, I expect.

BILLY. Well, I'm going to bed.

PHOEBE. Going already?

BILLY (*going to his room*). Yes, I only sat up to drink a toast to young Mick. I'm going to bed before you get those bloody Poles up here. Good night, everybody.
(*They all call out "good night".*)

PHOEBE. I suppose I ought to go in a minute. I feel a bit tired. Still, I shan't go in to work tomorrow. Well, I shouldn't think they'll expect me to, would you?

JEAN. Of course not.

PHOEBE. Probably be too excited to sleep anyway. (*To* JEAN.) Did I show you the letter I had from Clare?

JEAN. Who's Clare?

ARCHIE (*to* PHOEBE). I should go to bed, dear.

PHOEBE. Just a minute. I'm going to show her Clare's letter. Clare's my niece—that's the one in Toronto. I'd better read it to you, her writing's not very good. She's my brother John's daughter. They're all over there now, my brother, John, as well. They started off in the restaurant business four years ago with five hundred dollars— that's their little girl. (*Hands photograph to* JEAN.) Now they've got a hotel in Toronto, and they're going to open another one.

ARCHIE (*to* JEAN). You don't have to look interested, dear. (*To* PHOEBE.) She's not interested in all that horse manure about Canada.

PHOEBE. Of course she's interested. She doesn't mind listening, do you?

ARCHIE. Why doesn't Frank sing another song?

PHOEBE. I'm only trying to explain to her. They've opened one in Toronto, and now they're going to open another hotel in Ottawa. My brother, John, is managing the one in Toronto for them, but they want us to go out there, and for Archie to manage the hotel in Ottawa.

ARCHIE. What do I know about hotels? All I've lived in is digs.

PHOEBE. He gets cross if I mention it.

ARCHIE. For God's sake don't say I get cross if you mention it once more. You've mentioned it, haven't you? And I'm not cross! I just think it's a bloody pointless idea.

JEAN. When did they write this to you?

PHOEBE. About a fortnight now. Oh, she says we needn't make a decision for another month or two.

JEAN. What about the boys?

PHOEBE. They can come, too, if they want. I don't know about Mick, but Frank likes the idea, don't you?

JEAN. Do you, Frank?

FRANK. Look around you. Can you think of any good reason for staying in this cosy little corner of Europe? Don't kid yourself anyone's going to let you do anything, or try anything here, Jeannie. Because they're not. You haven't got a chance. Who are you—you're nobody. You're nobody, you've no money, and you're young. And when you end up it's pretty certain you'll still be nobody, you'll still have no money—the only difference is you'll be *old!* You'd better start thinking about number one, Jeannie, because nobody else is going to do it for you. Nobody else is going to do it for you because nobody believes in that stuff any more. Oh, they may say they do, and may take a few bob out of your pay packet every week and stick some stamps on your card to prove it, but don't believe it—nobody will give you a second look. They're all so busy, speeding down the middle of the road together, not giving a damn where they're going, as long as they're in the bloody middle! (*Chirpily, almost singing.*) *The rotten bastards!* "Oh, when there isn't a girl about you feel so lonely. When there isn't a girl about you're on your only."

ARCHIE. Ssh, you'll wake up the Poles.

FRANK. Somebody should wake you up. "You're on your only!"

ARCHIE. You should go to bed.

FRANK. You and that blonde bitch in the Cambridge. You and her.

ARCHIE. I could do her with a blunt instrument, all right.

FRANK. Like a monkey up a tree, I don't think! I'm going to bed.

    (*He goes out singing, laying an arm on* ARCHIE'S *shoulder, and waving to the others.*)

ARCHIE. Good night, boy.

FRANK (*singing*). "Rock of ages cleft for me,
  Let me hide myself in thee!"

(Exit.)

ARCHIE. Anyway, you can't buy draught Bass in Toronto.

PHOEBE. Here, this is what she says: she talks about us coming out, and paying our fare, etc., and then the job in Ottawa.. Experience isn't necessary, it's having your own people. She says: "We have a twenty-one inch T.V. set, a radio, etc., and now we have a 195— Chevrolet Bel Air car complete with automatic shift and all the fancy gadgets everyone goes in for over here. I'm quite sure that you and Archie would settle down in no time, and everything would work out fine". (*She folds the letter up carefully.*) I thought you'd like to hear what she said.

JEAN. Yes, thank you.

PHOEBE (*after a slight pause*). Are you staying up much longer, Archie?

ARCHIE. I'm just going.

PHOEBE. I think we're all tired. I can't take all this excitement any more. (*To* JEAN.) Good night, dear. Forgive me being a bit silly, won't you?

JEAN. Forget it. Good night. I shan't wake you up.

PHOEBE. Good night, Archie.

ARCHIE. I'll come up and say good night.

PHOEBE. Thank you, dear. We'll have to find him somewhere to sleep, won't we?

ARCHIE. Mick? Oh, he can bed down here with me.

PHOEBE. Yes, I expect he'll be fagged out, poor kid. Oh, well, he won't be long now. (*Exit.*)

ARCHIE. I went to Canada during the war.

JEAN. I remember.

ARCHIE. Couldn't get any draught Bass, not even in Toronto, and they seemed to reckon that was pretty English. (*Pause.*) Didn't seem very English to me. Can't get over you going to Trafalgar Square. Did you really care about all that?

JEAN. I thought I did at the time.

ARCHIE. Like draught Bass and women, eh? Couldn't get draught Bass anywhere. Plenty of women. Did I ever tell you how I got out of the army?

JEAN. No, I don't think so.

ARCHIE. I will, anyway. I like talking at this time of night. Anyway, I'm slewed. You don't mind hearing the same old stories, do you?

JEAN. No, I don't mind.

ARCHIE. Everybody tells you the same story. Well, I was making tea at the time, in the army, I mean. Lance-Corporal Rice—and that was my contribution to the war effort, making the tea. They wouldn't let anyone else do it. It's the truth, really. I know you don't believe me—never mind. Anyway, after a while I'd made up my mind that Archie was for getting out. There are ways of getting out, you know. Well, you probably do know, but there are ways. One way is to make out you're off your chump. That's pretty difficult. Only ever met one chap who got away with that, and he was, anyway. There's only really one other way. Yes, that can be difficult, too, believe it or not. Why they ever made it a reason for giving you your ticket, I could never quite understand. Doesn't make much sense, does it? Well, a chap who was in the billet with me was posted suddenly. He'd just got married, and, naturally, he was upset about it. So I went to the C.O. and asked if I could take his place. Did I ever tell you my nun's story? They just took one look at me—I can remember their white, unhealthy faces, and their little eyes—they took one look at me, and, together, at the same time, quite, quite, spontaneously, they crossed themselves. They crossed themselves. And that was the biggest compliment I ever had paid to me in my whole life. Let's have some more of this, shall we?

JEAN. Sure. Tell me about the C.O.

ARCHIE. The C.O., oh, yes. Well, I explained this chap was just married, and could I go in his place. And he said: "But, but you— you make the tea". So—I explained—I could train somebody else in the time. Then he lost interest a bit—I think you're losing interest really. What are you thinking?

JEAN. I'm not losing interest. I promise you I'm not losing interest.

ARCHIE. So he just said: "All right, Rice, if you can train somebody else properly in the time, you can go. But not otherwise, of course". And that's how I got to Canada. I think I like my nun's story better.

JEAN. And didn't you like Canada?

ARCHIE. Well, I went because I thought the Government was paying for it, but there was nothing there for anyone like me. They'd already got somebody making the tea, and I told you about the draught Bass, didn't I? You needn't worry. I'm used to not getting laughs. So after a couple of weeks I decided Archie was going to work his ticket. I ended up in front of a psychiatrist with a picture of Freud on the wall behind him as big as a Michael Angelo. He knew about as much about Freud as poor old Phoebe. "Of course," he said, "we're not used to dealing with your type of case over here." He was a Canadian, or an American, I think. "We've always considered this to be a European vice." European vice—and that's how Archie got his ticket. And the worse performance I ever gave. You were having trouble with Phoebe tonight?

JEAN. It was nothing much. She just seemed to suddenly turn on me.

ARCHIE. Your mother caught me in bed with Phoebe. (*Pause.*)

JEAN. I didn't know that.

ARCHIE. I don't know what I really expected, but somehow I expected you to say something more than that.

JEAN. What do you expect me to do—hold a rally in Trafalgar Square?

ARCHIE. All my children think I'm a bum. I've never bothered to hide it, I suppose—that's the answer.

JEAN. Perhaps we should go to bed.

ARCHIE. No, stay up for a while. I think we're both in the mood. You'd just been born and your mother found poor old Phoebe and me together. Poor old Phoebe, she's never even enjoyed it much. Your mother walked out, she walked out just like that. She was what you'd call a person of—a person of principle. She knew how people should behave, and there were no two ways about it. She never forgave me, anyway.

JEAN. You didn't love her—

　　(ARCHIE *is drunk, and he sings and orchestrates his speech as only a drunken man can, almost objectively and fastidiously, like a conductor controlling his own sound.*)

ARCHIE. Yes, I loved her. I was in love with her, whatever that may mean. I don't know. Anyway, a few months later she was dead and that was that. She felt everything very deeply, your mother. Much more deeply than I did. Perhaps we could have worked it out between us. She'd never been poor and lonely, or oppressed, but somehow, in some strange peculiar way of her own, she could feel things that were done to her. Do you know the most moving thing that I ever heard? It was when I was in Canada—I managed to slip over the border sometimes to some people I knew, and one night I heard some negress singing in a bar. *Now you're going to smile at this,* you're going to smile your educated English head off, because I suppose you've never sat lonely and half slewed in some bar among strangers a thousand miles from anything you think you understand. But if ever I saw any hope or strength in the human race, it was in the face of that old fat negress getting up to sing about Jesus or something like that. She was poor and lonely and oppressed like nobody you've ever known. Or me, for that matter. I never even liked that kind of music, but to see that old black whore singing her heart out to the whole world, you knew somehow in your heart that it didn't matter how much you kick people, the real people, how much you despise them, if they can stand up and make a pure, just natural noise like that, there's nothing wrong with them, only with everybody else. I've never heard anything like that since. I've never heard it here. Oh, I've heard whispers of it on a Saturday night somewhere. Oh, he's heard it. Billy's heard it. He's heard them singing. Years ago, poor old gubbins. But you won't hear it anywhere now. I don't suppose we'll ever hear it again. There's nobody who can feel like that. I wish to God I could, I wish to God I could feel like that old black bitch with her fat cheeks, and sing. If I'd done one thing as good as that in my whole life, I'd have been all right. Better than all your getting on with the job without making a fuss, or doing something constructive and all that, all your rallies in Trafalgar Square! I wish to God I were that old bag. I'd stand up and shake my great bosom up and down, and lift up my head and make the most beautiful fuss in the world. Dear God, I would.

But I'll never do it. I don't give a damn about anything, not even
women or draught Bass. Do you think that you're going to do it?
Well, do you?

JEAN. I don't know. I just really don't know. I'll probably do exactly
the same as you.

ARCHIE. Of course you will. Mind you, you'll make a better job of it.
You're more clever, I think you really feel something, too, in spite
of all that Trafalgar Square stuff. You're what they call a sentimen-
talist. You carry all your responses about with you, instead of
leaving them at home. While everyone else is sitting on their hands
you're the Joe at the back cheering and making his hands hurt.
But you'll have to sit on your hands like everyone else. Oh, you
think I'm just a tatty old music hall actor who should be told the
truth, like old Billy, that people don't wear sovereign cases and
patent leather shoes any more. You think you love all those people
around you out there, but you don't. You don't love them, you're
not going to stand up and make a beautiful fuss. If you learn it
properly you'll get yourself a technique. You can smile, darn you,
smile, and look the friendliest, jolliest thing in the world, but you'll
be just as dead and smug and used up, and sitting on your hands
just like everybody else. You see this face, you see this face, this face
can split open with warmth and humanity. It can sing, and tell
the worst, unfunniest stories in the world to a great mob of dead,
drab erks and it doesn't matter, it doesn't matter. It doesn't matter
because—look at my eyes. I'm dead behind these eyes. I'm dead,
just like the whole inert, shoddy lot out there. It doesn't matter
because I don't feel a thing, and neither do they. We're just as
dead as each other. Tell me, tell me something. I want you to tell
me something. What would you say to a man of my age marrying
a girl of—oh, about your age? Don't be shocked. I told you—I
don't feel a thing.

JEAN. You couldn't, you really couldn't! You couldn't do a thing
like that!

ARCHIE. You've been away from your old Dad a bit too long. We've
never seen much of each other, have we? Well, never mind.

JEAN. You're not serious! You couldn't do that to Phoebe—not a
divorce!

ARCHIE. Children! (*Laughs.*) Children! They're like the bloody
music hall. Don't worry about your old man—he's still a bit worried

about young Mick. At least, I suppose he is. I told you, nothing really touches me. As the man said, I've paid me one and saxpence— I defy yez to entertain me! Let anyone get up there and give a performance, let them get up. I don't care how good it is. Old Archie, dead behind the eyes, is sitting on his hands, he lost his responses on the way. You wouldn't think I was sexy to look at me, would you? Well, I 'ave a go, lady. I 'ave a go, don't I? I do. I 'ave a go. That barmaid in the Cambridge. That barmaid who upset poor old Billy in the Cambridge—I had her! When he wasn't looking—

(*Enter* PHOEBE, R.)

PHOEBE. I thought you'd got somebody here. They called up from downstairs. There's a policeman at the door for you, Archie.

ARCHIE. It's the income tax man. It's the income tax man. Tell him I've been expecting him. I've been expecting him for twenty years.

PHOEBE (*to* JEAN). I thought he had someone in here. What do you think he wants?

ARCHIE. Just me and my daughter Jean. Me and my daughter Jean— by my first love. Why don't you go back to London? Say, aren't you glad you're normal? Well, it's everybody's problem. Unless you're like Mick and have got no problem. Well, he had a problem, but now he's on his way. Yes, that's a boy without problems. Poor old Phoebe, don't look so scared, love. Either they're doing it, and they're not enjoying it. Or else they're not doing it and they aren't enjoying it. Don't look so scared, love. Archie's drunk again. It's only the income tax man!

PHOEBE. Frank's down there—

(FRANK *bursts in.*)

FRANK. The bastards! *The rotten bastards!* They've killed him! They've killed Mick! Oh, the rotten bastards! Those bloody wogs, they've murdered him!

ARCHIE (*slowly singing the blues*). Oh, lord, I don't care where they bury my body, no I don't care where they bury my body, 'cos my soul's going to live with God!

CURTAIN

NUMBER NINE

Blues. Spot on FRANK, *piano.*

FRANK. Bring back his body, and bury it in England
So bring back his body, and bury it here.
Bring back his body, in an aeroplane,
But don't ever talk to me.
Those playing fields of Eton
Have really got us beaten.
But ain't no use agrievin'
Cos it's Britain we believe in.
So bring back his body, and bury it here.
Oh, bring back his body in an aeroplane—
But just don't ever talk to me. *(Ad lib.)*

FADE

NUMBER TEN

BILLY, PHOEBE, JEAN, FRANK *and* ARCHIE. BILLY *and* PHOEBE
are dressed in black. The others wear black arm bands.

JEAN. Well, that's that. *(Picks up some newspapers.)* Can anyone tell
me what the whole thing added up to? *(Pause.)*

ARCHIE. My aunt always used to say the same thing: "Well, they gave
him a good send-off". Always said it without fail. *(To* BILLY.*)*
Didn't she?

BILLY. Poor old Rosie.

ARCHIE. I used to wonder what would happen if she didn't say it.

BILLY. Old Rosie and me used to have good times together. Used
to go out a lot. Before we were both married.

JEAN. Well, I suppose it gives somebody a kick. Are you all right,
Phoebe?

PHOEBE. I'm all right, dear. A bit tired.

BILLY. What a place London was then for having a good time. Best
place in the world for a laugh. People were always ready to laugh,
to give you a welcome. Best audience in the world.

ARCHIE. I was in a little village in Donegal once. On the Irish fit-ups.
(To BILLY.*)* You remember. The morning we arrived there, a

man came up to me and said: "Oh, we're great students of the drama here. Great students of the drama. Our dramatic critic can lick anyone—anyone!" Turned out he was the local blacksmith. He said, he said: "If you get past an audience here, you'll get past any audience in the world". It was true, too. Think I got a black eye.

BILLY. Some places, they just sit back and stare at you. They just—sit. But, London, that was the place. Old Rosie—she was a beautiful woman. I'm glad she's not here now.

JEAN (*grabbing at newspapers*). How can you compete against this stuff?

FRANK. You can't.

JEAN. Why didn't somebody get a picture of you stoking your boilers?

ARCHIE. I don't think Mick would have taken it too seriously.

FRANK. Everybody's tired.

JEAN. Everybody's tired all right. Everybody's tired, everybody's standing about, loitering without any intent whatsoever, waiting to be picked up by whatever they may allow to happen to us next.

ARCHIE. Jesus, don't start getting emotional—

JEAN. I don't expect you to.

ARCHIE. That's right.

JEAN. But Frank's different—at least, I hope he is. You don't have to be afraid, Frank. You needn't worry about being emotional, like my talented *fiancé*. You won't die of it. You may think you can, but you won't.

ARCHIE. Old Mick was a bit like Graham, actually. He seemed to know what he wanted, and where he was going.

JEAN. Did he now, that's interesting—

ARCHIE. I remember he was having an affair with a girl called Sylvia. He was about sixteen at the time.

JEAN. What's the matter with you, Archie?

ARCHIE. Went out for a walk on his own—afterwards.

FRANK. Why don't you leave him alone?

ARCHIE. That's right, why don't you leave your old man alone?

JEAN. Oh, you've been left alone all right!

ARCHIE. Shall I tell you? All my life I've been searching for something. I've been searching for a draught Bass you can drink all the evening without running off to the loo every ten minutes, that you can get drunk on without feeling sick, and all for fourpence. Now, the man who could offer me all of that would really get my vote. He really

T.E.—E

would.   Oh, well, I could always make a woman better than I
could make a point.

JEAN. You know, Archie, you're a bit of a bastard.

PHOEBE. Jean—

JEAN. You really are—you're a bastard on wheels!

ARCHIE. Because I don't care about anything except draught Bass?
Listen, kiddie, you're going to find out that in the end nobody
really gives a damn about anything except some little animal
something.   And for me that little animal something is draught
Bass.   Now why can't you stop attacking everyone?

JEAN. I can't.

ARCHIE. What do you think you are—a dose of salts?

JEAN. I owe it to myself.

ARCHIE.   Well, I never really believed in all that inner cleanliness,
anyway.   Did I leave a bottle of beer in here last night?

PHOEBE. I don't think so, dear.

ARCHIE. If you're not careful, Jean, people will start putting labels
on you pretty soon.   And then you'll just be nobody.   You'll be
nobody like the rest of us.

PHOEBE. Frank'll get you some.   There's some left in the kitchen.
Would you mind, dear?

FRANK. Sure.

JEAN. We can't all spend our time nailing our suitcases to the floor,
and shin out of the window.

ARCHIE. Scarper the letty.

JEAN. You're like everybody else, but you're worse—you think you
can cover yourself by simply not bothering; you're swinging the
lead, you want make-believe, you want all this stuff. (*Newspapers.*)
You think if you don't bother you can't be humiliated, so you just
roar your life out in four-letter words and just hope that somehow
the perks will turn up.

FRANK. Leave him alone, he's just as upset as you are!   So shut up.

JEAN. I'll give you the Archie Rice story.   All right.   You want the
credit titles first?

ARCHIE. I didn't like the clergyman, anyway.   I really hated him.   He
was as chloe as all get out.   Did you notice?

JEAN. You don't fool me.   You couldn't fool pussy!

ARCHIE. Go on—insult me, I don't mind.   One thing I've discovered
a long time ago.   Most people never know when they're being

insulted. And a whole lot of people make a whole lot of money out of that principle. I'm as dim as a bucket, really, you know. I'm no better than the rest of them.

JEAN. Oh now, don't start being humble—

ARCHIE. I *am* humble! I am very humble, in fact. I still have a little dried pea of humility rattling around inside me. I don't think *you* have.

JEAN. And that's just about all.

FRANK. What's the matter with her?

ARCHIE. Don't ask me, son. Don't ask me. I've never solved a problem in my life.

JEAN. You haven't got the nous. You've been too busy hating those feckless moochers out there in the great darkness all these years. You've been really smart. (*To* FRANK.) I'd like you to know the truth about your father.

FRANK. Listen, Jean, Mick's just been buried. He's buried and nobody wants to start talking about it, or having rows.

JEAN. What do you want, two minutes' silence? Not only is your father generous, understanding and sympathetic—he doesn't give a care about anyone. He's two pennorth of nothing.

ARCHIE. Yes, I should say that sums me up pretty well.

JEAN. You don't need to look at me! I've lost a brother, too. I just want to know what this whole thing's about. Why do people like us sit here, and just lap it all up, why do boys die, or stoke boilers, why do we pick up these things, what are we hoping to get out of it, what's it all in aid of—is it really for the sake of a gloved hand waving at you from a golden coach?

PHOEBE. I think I'll go and lie down. (*To* JEAN.) He's always been good to us.

FRANK. Shall I bring you up an aspirin?

JEAN. Nobody listens to anyone.

PHOEBE. Thank you, dear. If you wouldn't mind. (*To* JEAN, *simply*.) He's always been good to me. Whatever he may have done. Always. (*Exit* R.)

FRANK. I'll get you that beer.

BILLY. Always a decanter on the sideboard at home. I've got the key here.

JEAN (*to* ARCHIE). You can't do it to her, I won't let you.

BILLY. Yes, here it is.

ARCHIE. He wants to know if I've renewed the ticket. It's all right—
I've got another three months on it.

BILLY. Eh? (*To* JEAN.) There.

JEAN. What's this?

BILLY. What's the matter—you want your bloody ears syringed?

FRANK. You want some beer, Grandad?

BILLY. Nobody listens to a bloody word you're saying.

FRANK. I said do you want some beer?

BILLY. That's the trouble nowadays. Everybody's too busy answering
back and taking liberties, 'stead of getting on with it and doing as
they're told. No, I'm going to bed. I've got to be out early tomorrow. (*To* ARCHIE.) What time did you say?

ARCHIE. About nine.

FRANK. Where are you going?

BILLY. Your father and I have got some business together. Seemed
funny all those people taking off their hats to young Mick today.

FRANK. Most of 'em weren't wearing hats, anyway.

BILLY. When I was younger, every man—and every man wore a
hat in those days, didn't matter if he was a lord or a butcher—
every man used to take his hat off when he passed the Cenotaph.
Even in the bus. Nowadays I've watched people just go past it, not
even a look. If you took the flags off of it I expect they'd sit down
and eat their sandwiches on it. I don't know—you read all the time
about people being clothes-conscious and sex-conscious, why the
other day I read in the paper that in America they're even becoming
radiation-conscious. If you ask me half of them are just plain bloody
*un*conscious.

ARCHIE. I was just thinking of young Mick and Sylvia. She was a
nice, attractive little kid. I wonder what she's doing now. I wonder
if she's read about him in the papers. I shouldn't think she'd have
forgotten him already, would you?

FRANK. I shouldn't think so. Can I have some of your beer?

ARCHIE. Help yourself. I remember being worried about Sylvia. I
couldn't get it out of young Mick, and I had an idea she was under-
age. It worried me just a bit. I tried to tackle him about it, but he
always thought I was a bit of a chump, he did, you know. Oh,
I didn't mind. I rather liked it. (*To* JEAN.) He didn't really take me
seriously. I hummed and hah'ed, and finally I said: "Well, look boy,
I obviously don't have to tell you to take precautions". He just

grinned like the clappers, and I suddenly felt like some weird old clergyman. So I just said to him: "Well, anyway, you do know what the age of consent is, don't you?" And he sat there with that great awful grin on his face, and said: "Sixteen".

JEAN. Where are you taking Billy tomorrow?

ARCHIE. I think I'll have to go back to Brighton, and become a beachcomber.

FRANK (*to* JEAN). Got any aspirins on you? There don't seem to be any.

ARCHIE. Edlins—that was the place. All over Brighton.

JEAN (*giving* FRANK *aspirins*). Don't you know what he's trying to do?

ARCHIE. You could get nicely oiled up to the eyebrows on their draught cider for a few pence.

FRANK. Why don't you leave them alone?

ARCHIE. Haven't had it for years. How much was it?

JEAN. He thinks he's going to divorce her. He thinks he's going to divorce Phoebe. I've seen her—this girl he wants to marry. He's crazy. That's what he is. What's going to happen to her? (*She nods upstairs.*)

FRANK. What's going to happen to any of us? Listen, Jean, love— darling heart, you are not going to change anybody—

JEAN. Have you seen her? I caught them together yesterday. In the Rockcliffe. I've seen her all right. She's a professional virgin.

FRANK. I'd better take these (*Aspirins.*) up to her.

ARCHIE. I wonder what it's like now. (*To* BILLY.) How much did it used to be?

BILLY. What?

ARCHIE. Draught cider, you old gubbins.

BILLY. How the bloody hell should I know? I've never drunk the stuff.

ARCHIE. Yes, it's a bit acid, I suppose.

BILLY. 'bout a penny, I should say. Penny a pint.

ARCHIE. Be about a bob now, I 'spect. (*Slight pause.*) Might as well drink beer.

JEAN (*to* ARCHIE). She's pretty, she's spoilt, she's vain, and she's stupid. And her parents are probably stupid. They must be, they must be stupid to produce her—Miss Nothing of nineteen fifty—.

ARCHIE. That's right.

JEAN. How old is she?

ARCHIE. Twenty.

JEAN. Twenty. They're so stupid, I suppose, they'll even let her marry you.

ARCHIE.   You know, I think I've only slept with one passionate woman. What I'd call really passionate. And she was happily married. Her name was Ivy.

JEAN.   I suppose you think you'll get them to put up some money for you, too?

ARCHIE.   That was the idea.

JEAN.   You're going to get her to put a ring through your nose, and tell yourself you won't fee! it, because nothing matters to you any more, and nobody else does either. You think because you can't get her, nobody else can! What about Phoebe?

ARCHIE.   Ivy Williams, that's her name. Mrs. Ivy Williams. Mrs. Ivy Williams.

BILLY.   Well, I'm off. Who're we seeing: Rubens?

ARCHIE.   Klein.

BILLY.   Charlie Klein. Old Charlie Klein. I was in the first show he ever put on the road, you know that?

ARCHIE.   Twelve-thirty.

BILLY.   He was younger than Jeannie here. I made him a member of the National Sporting Club. It was me who put him up.

ARCHIE.   He's a tough bastard.

BILLY.   Oh, Charlie should be all right. It was me made him sign up Eddie Drummer. Good artist, Eddie. Been earning a thousand a week for twenty-five years, and just the same. He's a good boy. He's a sort of in-between. He wasn't one of us real old timers, and he wasn't one of these new five-minute wonders with a microphone. They've got no real personality now. He always had style, Eddie, and never any real suggestion of offence in anything he did. We all had our own style, our own songs—and we were all English. What's more, we spoke English. Why, they don't even know how to make-up. I used to take an hour and a half over my make-up every night. An hour and a half. It was different. We all knew what the rules were. We knew what the rules were, and even if we spent half our time making people laugh at 'em we never serious-ly suggested that anyone should break them. A real pro is a real man, all he needs is an old back cloth behind him and he can hold them on his own for half an hour. He's like the general run of people, only he's a lot more like them than they are themselves, if you understand me. Well, Eddie's still up there all right. He's still up there. (*To* JEAN.) I always used to say to him, we all used to say: "Eddie—always be good to the people on the way up, because you may meet them on the way down". Old Eddie. One of the really great ones, I should say he is. I should say he's probably the last. Yes, I should say he's probably the last. (*Exit* R.)

JEAN. What are you doing, what are you going to do to him? You're not going to put him back into the business.

ARCHIE. Rubens and Klein twelve-thirty tomorrow morning—

JEAN. You're going to kill that old man just to save that no-good, washed-up tatty show of yours—

ARCHIE. It isn't just to save that no-good tatty show of mine. It's to save your no-good tatty Dad from going to jail. People may not come to see Archie but they may still remember Billy Rice. It's worth a try, anyway.

JEAN. Are you going to destroy that, too? He's the only one of us who has any dignity or respect for himself, he's the only one of us who has anything at all, and you're going to murder him, you're going to take him down to—who is it?—Rubens and Klein tomorrow morning at twelve-thirty, and you're going to let Mr. Rubens and Mr. Klein sign his death certificate. What are you letting yourself in for now, how on earth did you ever get him to do such a thing? What's happened to him? What's happened to his sense of self preservation?

ARCHIE. He feels he owes it to me.

JEAN. Owes it to you! Owes it to you! Billy doesn't owe you or anyone anything.

ARCHIE. You see, while you were busy lecturing me about inner cleanliness, Billy went and did something. He went and saw my little girl friend's parents, you know, the professional virgin you saw in the Rockcliffe. He went and told them I was a married man with three grown-up children. Three acknowledged—anyway, but I don't suppose old Billy needed to mention the rest of them.

JEAN. He scotched it!

ARCHIE. Oh, yes—completely. You see, I hadn't told them about—about Phoebe, and all of you.

JEAN. No, I suppose you wouldn't.

ARCHIE. So you see you weren't wrong, Jeannie, love. Not about Phoebe anyway—old Archie isn't going to get his oats after all.

CURTAIN

NUMBER ELEVEN

Darkened stage. The voice of a negress singing slowly: "I must tell Jesus". *Spot on* ARCHIE *on prompt side.*

ARCHIE. Ladies and Gentlemen, Billy Rice will not appear tonight. Billy Rice will not appear again. I wish I could sing a song for him —in his place. A farewell. But, unfortunately, I can't. Nobody can. None of us, anyway.

Spot fades.

Music comes up. During ARCHIE'S *short speech four stage hands have carried on a coffin behind the front gauze. It is covered by a flag,* BILLY'S *hat, gloves and cane.* ARCHIE, PHOEBE, FRANK *and* JEAN *do this. They are followed by* GRAHAM *and* BROTHER BILL.

Suddenly a spot hits a rostrum above where the coffin has been laid, revealing a negress, miming to the music. She goes into a dance, putting on the hat, the gloves, and carrying the cane, stripping off the flag. (The whole number, including ARCHIE, *takes exactly three minutes.)*

FADE

NUMBER TWELVE

A chair D.L. *A lime drenches* ARCHIE *and* BROTHER BILL. *A chair* D.R. *and a lime on* JEAN *and* GRAHAM DODD. BROTHER BILL *looks like a highly successful and distinguished lawyer, and he is.* GRAHAM DODD *may well be like him in thirty years, provided he is successful. There are plenty of these around—well dressed, assured, well educated, their emotional and imaginative capacity so limited it is practically negligible. They have an all-defying inability to associate themselves with anyone in circumstances even slightly dissimilar to their own. No.* GRAHAM DODD *doesn't need much description. If you can't recognize him, it's for one reason only. These two duologues are independent, but run together.*

GRAHAM. Quite honestly, Jean, I don't mean to be rude. I mean, well it is rude to come out and say it, but I can't see what you can possibly have in common with any of them.

JEAN. You can't—

GRAHAM. Well, they're your family and all that, but after all, there does come a point, there does come a point in things—

ARCHIE. He was such a sweet old man. He really was. D'you know who said that? Charlie Klein. Charlie Klein said old Billy was the nicest old man in the business.

GRAHAM. —you just don't have any more responsibility to people.

ARCHIE. And still a first-class performer, Archie. Still a first-class performer!

GRAHAM. —it's your background and you were brought up in it, but there are better, more worthwhile things in life.

ARCHIE. He was one of the great, one of the really great.

JEAN. I'm sorry, Graham, I'm staying with Phoebe. I told you I'd really made up my mind before I left. I can't marry you, and I don't want to any more. Anyway, I've got to stay here. Now that Billy's dead Phoebe needs someone with her. Frank's off to Canada in a couple of weeks—

ARCHIE. Jean thinks I killed him.

BROTHER BILL. You didn't kill him, Archie. You don't kill people that easily. I don't think so.

JEAN. We live differently. You and I don't even draw breath in the same way.

BROTHER BILL. Look, Archie. This is the last time for you. It's got to be Canada. You and Frank and Phoebe can all go out together. Your passages are all booked. I've got them in my pocket here. They're yours. You can go out and start a new life, the three of you.

GRAHAM. Oh, this is just rubbish. You're no different from me. You were in love with me, you said so. We enjoyed ourselves together. We could make a good thing of it. I've got quite a decent career lined up. We would have everything we want. Come back with me, Jean.

ARCHIE. You can't get draught Bass in Toronto. I've tried it.

JEAN. Have you ever got on a railway train here, got on a train from Birmingham to West Hartlepool. Or go from Manchester to Warrington or Widnes. And you get out, you go down the street, and on one side maybe is a chemical works, and on the other is the railway goods yard. Some kids are playing in the street, and you walk up to some woman standing on her doorstep. It isn't a doorstep really because you can walk straight from the street into her front room. What can you say to her. What real piece of informa-

tion, what message can you give to her? Do you say: "Madam,
d'you know that Jesus died on the Cross for you"?

BROTHER BILL. Those tickets are yours, Archie. Now take them. I'll
pay up all your debts, I'll settle everything, I'll see that nothing
happens.

JEAN. And then the woman, she looks back at you, and she says:
"Oh, yes, I heard all about that".

ARCHIE. What happens if I don't go?

BROTHER BILL. I'm not doing anything for you to stay here, Archie.
Not any more. You'll just have to take the consequences, I'm afraid.

ARCHIE. You know, I've always thought I should go to jail. I should
think it must be quite interesting. Sure to meet someone I know.
D'you know what my landlady in Fulham used to say about you?
She used to say: "He looks like a gov'nor's man". Always said it—
without fail.

GRAHAM. We're all in it for what we can get out of it. Isn't that what
your father was supposed to say?

ARCHIE. You can never get anything at this Labour Exchange, anyway.
They must have more bums in this place than in any other town in
England. Oh, well, just two more performances. It's a pity though
—I should have liked to notch up twenty-one against the income
tax man. I'll never make my twenty-first now. It would have been
fun to get the key of the door, somehow.

JEAN. Here we are, we're alone in the universe, there's no God; it
just seems that it all began by something as simple as sunlight striking
on a piece of rock. And here we are. We've only got ourselves.
Somehow, we've just got to make a go of it. *We've only ourselves.*

BROTHER BILL. I'm sorry, Archie, but I've given up trying to understand.

FADE

NUMBER THIRTEEN

*Rock-n-roll. Nude tableau behind first act gauze. Britannia.
Then: the Archie Rice Music, the one and only, interrupting the
programme. The stage blacks out. A lime picks out the prompt corner,
and* ARCHIE *makes his entrance. He sings a few bars of* "We're all
out for good old Number One".

ARCHIE. We're all out for good old Number One
  Number One's the only one for me.
  Good old England, you're my cup of tea,
  But I don't want no drab equality.
  Don't let your feelings roam
  But remember that charity begins at home.
  For Britons shall be free!
  For Britons shall be free!
  What we've got left back
  We'll keep, and blow you, Jack!
  Number One's the only one for me.

I've just come to tell you about the wife. She's gone back to her
husband. She has, straight. Don't clap too hard, we're all in a very
old building. Yes, very old. Old. What about *that?* What about
her, eh—Madam with the helmet on? I reckon she's sagging a bit,
if you ask me. She needs some beef putting into her—the roast
beef of Old England. No, nobody's asking me, never mind. Nice
couple of fried eggs, anyway. She's a nice girl, though—a nice girl.
Going steady with Charlie here—isn't she, Charlie? (*To the conductor.*) She met him in a revolving door and they've been going around
together ever since. I'm doing me nut, you know that, don't you?
I'm doing me nut up here. Nudes, that's what they call them, lady,
nudes. Blimey, she's got more clothes on than I have. It's a lot of
madam, that's all it is. A lot of madam. Oh, I put a line in there.
Never mind, it doesn't matter. I've made a few tumbles in my time.
I have, honest. You wouldn't think I was sexy to look at me, would
you? No, honestly, you wouldn't, would you, lady? I always
reckon you feel stronger after it. (*Sings.*) "Say your jelly-roll is
fine, but it don't compare with mine!" There's a bloke at the side
here with a hook, you know that, don't you? He is, he's standing
there. I can see him. Must be the income tax man. Life's funny
though, isn't it? It is—life's funny. It's like sucking a sweet with the
wrapper on. Oh, well, we're all in the fertilizer business now, I
suppose. Well, I'd rather have a glass of beer any day—I would.
You don't believe me, but I would. You think I'm gone, don't
you? Go on, say it, you think I'm gone. You think I'm gone,
don't you? Well, I am. What's the matter, you feeling cold up
there? Before I do go, ladies and gentlemen, I should just like to
tell you a little story, a little story. This story is about a man, just

a little, ordinary man, like you and me, and one day he woke up and found himself in paradise. Well, he looks up, you see, and he sees a feller standing next to him. It turns out that this feller is a saint or something. Anyway, he's on the welcoming committee. And the feller says to him—the saint—says to him: "Well," he says, "you're now in paradise." "Am I?" he says. "You are," says the saint. "What's more, you have earned yourself eternal happiness." "Have I?" he says. "You most certainly have," says the saint. "Oh, you're well away," he says. "Can't you hear the multitudes?" "Why, everyone is singing, everyone is joyful. What do you say, my son?" So the little man took a look around him at all the multitudes of the earth, spread out against the universe. So he says to the saint: "Well, can I get up where you're standing, and take a proper look?" So the saint says: "Of course, you can, my son," and makes way for him. And the little man stood up where the saint was and gazed up at the sight around him. At all the Hosts of Heaven, and all the rest of it. "All the wonder and the joy of eternity is round about you," said the saint. "You mean, this is all eternity and I'm in paradise?" "That is so, my son. Well, what have you to say?" So the little man looks round again for a bit, and the saint says: "Well, my son?" "Well," he says, "I've often wondered what I'd say if this ever happened to me. I couldn't think somehow." And the saint smiled at him kindly and says again: "And what *do* you say, my son?" "Only one thing I can say," says the little man. (*He makes a whistling sound.*) Well, the saint looked as if he had been struck across the face by some great hand. The Hosts stopped singing and all the Angels hid their faces, and for a tiny splash in eternity there was no sound at all in paradise. The saint couldn't speak for a while, and then he threw his arms round the little man, and kissed him. And he said: "I love you, my son. With all my soul I shall love you always. I have been waiting to hear that ever since I came here." He's there with his little hook, I can see him. Oh, well, I have to go, don't I? I 'ave to go.

(*The cloth goes up, revealing a dark, bare stage. The music starts up softly, and* ARCHIE RICE *stands on the stage in a little round world of light, and swaggers gently into his song.*)
Why should I care
Why should I let it touch me,
Why shouldn't I sit down and try

To let it pass over me?

>   (*He begins to falter a little.*)

Why should—

Why should I let it get me?

What's the use of despair,

>   (*He stops and stares ahead of him. The music goes on, then he picks up.*)

If they see that you're blue

They'll look down on you

>   (PHOEBE *appears* L. *holding a raincoat and hat.*)

So why, oh why, should I bother to care?

> (*He stops, the music goes on, as he walks over to* PHOEBE, *who helps him on with his coat and gives him his hat. He hesitates, comes back down to the floats.*)

You've been a good audience. Very good. A very *good* audience. Let me know where you're working tomorrow night—and I'll come and see *you.*

> (*He walks* U.S. *with* PHOEBE. *The spotlight is hitting the apron, where* ARCHIE *has been standing. The orchestra goes on playing:* "Why should I care?" *Suddenly the little world of light snaps out, the stage is bare and dark.* ARCHIE RICE *has gone. There is only the music.*)

CURTAIN

PROPERTY LIST

ACT I

Overture

NO. 1 (BILLY and JEAN)
Dustbin, U.R. (against wall)
Chair, D.R., *on it:* rug
Table, U.R., *on it:* matches
Table, D.L., *on it:* two beer glasses, ashtray, *under it:* box for slippers
Armchair, D.L., *on it:* cushion, *under it:* slippers, *behind it:* waste paper basket
Door, U.R., *hanging on it:* coat hanger, clothes-brush, four coat hooks (permanent)
Floor, D.S., telegram and envelope
Room gauze, powder puff, mirror
Standard lamp, U.L.

NO. 2 (ARCHIE RICE—"Don't take him seriously")
In front of nude gauze and black tabs

NO. 3 (BILLY, JEAN and PHOEBE)
Round table, C., *on it:* new half-bottle gin, bottle lime squash
Two bentwood chairs, L. and R. of round table
Table, D.L., *on it:* two gin glasses (one taped), ashtray, evening paper, telegram
Table, D.R., *on it:* nail file, orange stick
Armchair, D.L., *behind it:* waste paper basket
Room gauze mirror, *in front of it:* powder puff
Door (ajar), *hanging on it:* Jean's coat, Billy's coat, hat, scarf
Standard lamp, U.L.

NO. 4 (ARCHIE RICE—"In trouble again")
As No. 2

NO. 5 (BILLY, JEAN, PHOEBE and ARCHIE)
Table, U.R., *on it:* one gin glass
Round table, C., *on it:* empty half-bottle gin, full beer glass, ashtray, knitting, two gin glasses
Armchair, D.L., *on arm:* evening paper, *behind it:* waste paper basket
Table, D.L., *on it:* lime bottle, gin glass, telegram
Room gauze, *on it:* powder puff, mirror
Two bentwood chairs, L. and R. of round table
Standard lamp, U.L.

INTERMISSION

NO. 6 (BILLY, PHOEBE, JEAN, ARCHIE and FRANK)
Round table, C., *on it:* three newspapers, gin bottle (quarter-full), three gin glasses, ashtray

Two bentwood chairs, R. and L. of round table, C.
Armchair, D.L., *on it:* two newspapers
Sofa, D.R., *on it:* one newspaper
Table, D.L., *on it:* four gin glasses, beer glass
Table, U.R., *on it:* lime bottle, bottle openers
Standard lamp, U.L.

NO. 7 (ARCHIE RICE—"Interrupts the programme")
As Nos. 2 and 4

NO. 8 (BILLY, PHOEBE, JEAN, ARCHIE and FRANK)
Table, U.R., *on it:* one used gin bottle, one new gin bottle, five gin glasses, one bottle Bass, bottle openers, Dubonnet bottle, quarter-full beer glass (for Jean)
Sofa, D.R., *on it:* newspaper
Round table, U.L., *on it:* pile gramophone records (two special), knitting needle, Phoebe's handbag, with photo of child and letter, ashtray, beer glass quarter-full
One bentwood chair, U.L. of round table
Step ladder, C., *on it:* gramophone (practical), lid open and plugged in to chandelier
Armchair, D.L.
Table, D.L.
Standard lamp, U.L.

INTERMISSION

NO. 9 (FRANK RICE—"Singing for you")
In front of black tabs closed

NO. 10 (BILLY, PHOEBE, JEAN, ARCHIE and FRANK)
Table, C., *on it:* two newspapers
Two bentwood chairs to L. and R. of round table
Sofa, D.R., *on it:* rug
Armchair, D.L.
Table, D.L.
Chair, U.L.
Standard lamp, U.L.
Table, U.R.

NO. 11 (ARCHIE)
Coffin

NO. 12 (JEAN and GRAHAM; ARCHIE and BROTHER BILL)
Stage bare except for tabs at side

NO. 13 (ARCHIE RICE—"The one and only")
Stage bare

OFFSTAGE

BOTTOM OF STAIRCASE, U.S.
    Suitcase containing packet cigars
    Carrier bag containing bottle gin and Dubonnet
    Carrier bag containing bottle gin and Dubonnet and *Daily Telegraph*,
        opened telegram
PROMPT SIDE TABLE
    Two pint bottles beer, evening paper, pint bottle beer, beer glass, small
        packet cigarettes, book matches, spectacles
    For Act III
    Black top hat, Billy's stick, cigar, grey gloves, Union Jack
O.P. SIDE TABLE
    Bentwood chair, new half-bottle gin
ORCHESTRA PIT
    Dummy violin bow
U.S.L.
    Coffin
IN NUDE'S CARRIAGE, R.
    Stuffed bulldog, trident, Union Jack

PERSONAL PROPS

BILLY
    Scarf, cane, purse with ten-shilling note inside, matches
JEAN
    Engagement ring, handbag with cigarettes, matches, aspirins, black armband
PHOEBE
    Black armband, handbag with picture post-card, photo of small child,
        letter from Canada
FRANK
    Cigarettes, matches, black armband
BROTHER BILL
    Umbrella, airline tickets to Canada
GRAHAM
    Umbrella, black armband
ARCHIE
    Black stick, two gold rings, silver watch, evening paper, new packet cigar-
        ettes, black armband

DRINKS NEEDED FOR EACH PERFORMANCE

Three new bottles gin without wrappers and foil turned back
Two bottles Dubonnet, unwrapped, one without foil, one foil turned back
Two half-bottles gin, fully wrapped
One bottle lime juice
One bottle gin, quarter-full
One half-bottle gin, empty
One bottle Bass
Three bottles pale ale (pint)

MADE AND PRINTED IN GREAT BRITAIN BY
LATIMER TREND & COMPANY LTD PLYMOUTH
MADE IN ENGLAND